Designing for Crafts

Designing for Crafts

XENIA LEY PARKER

CHARLES SCRIBNER'S SONS
NEW YORK

ACKNOWLEDGMENT

I would like to thank the many people who contributed to this book by their advice and their kindness in making available photographs of the selected works within: the artists and craftspeople, the private and public collectors, and the dedicated people of the museums, galleries and public agencies. I want to express a special note of thanks to my editor, Elinor Parker, for affording me the benefits of her patience and insight.

CREDITS

Outdoor photographs by Martin Parker. Photographs on pages 21, 38, 159, 163, 166, 169 taken by the author at Scarabaeus Gallery. Sketches by the author.

Library of Congress Cataloging in Publication Data

Parker, Xenia Ley.
Designing for Crafts.
Bibliography: p.
1. Handicraft. 2. Design. 3. Design, Decorative.
I. Title.
TT149.P37 745.5 74-2101
ISBN 0-684-13866-2

1 3 5 7 9 11 13 15 17 19 C/MD 20 18 16 14 12 10 8 6 4 2

Printed in the United States of America

Design by Angela Foote

Contents

TO CHRISTIANA

Introduction

DESIGN IS AN EVER-PRESENT FACTOR in our lives. It makes up the world we know and literally surrounds us in art, nature and industry. The smallest wood carving and the largest abstract painting share in common those basic principles of line, shape, mass, color and texture that can be found in leaves and locomotives.

These elements can be ordered on principles that have been known and used for centuries. They form a sensory alphabet with which you can translate the themes of your ideas into the structure of your work. These concepts are not difficult to master and are as necessary a part of the handcrafter's equipment as their needle, potter's wheel or loom.

Whether it is a study in stitchery, a ceramic vase or a marble bas relief, work at its best reflects a sense of originality and incorporates the nature of the materials into the design. Ideally, it presents an individual way of seeing and offers an insight into the conceptual image the artist tries to convey through craftsmanship by design.

As more creative people explore new forms of personal statement in the craft media, it becomes increasingly evident that the tools of design are a valuable addition to anyone's workbag. Each of us is unique; no two people perceive their surroundings or react to it in exactly the same way. It is this basic originality of viewpoint which should be cultivated and expressed to its fullest extent.

CHAPTER ONE

Design Itself

THERE ARE TWO GENERALLY ACCEPTED CONCEPTS of design, regarding any medium of expression. The first is structural, in that "form follows function," the well-known maxim that the shape of an article is predicated by its intended use. With this thought in mind, it can be said that objects that are physically suited to their purpose are endowed with their own special beauty.

The second concept is decorative and usually refers to the ornamentation or other pattern that is applied to the surface of an object to make it more stimulating to the eye.

These two elements are so inseparable that they can become as interchangeable as the word design itself. A plate can be made with a specified diameter and thickness and result in a fine receptacle for foods of all sorts. But if we want to include a surface design, it becomes such an integral part that it is best planned keeping the other characteristics and uses of the plate in mind.

Merely adding decoration to an object will not work. A successful design is planned from the first, to complement the functional requirements and enhance them as well.

In designing for crafts, the two basic concepts should be considered simultaneously whenever possible. In many cases, you will find that the functional aspects of an article are fairly well defined. Then, you will want to plan a surface design that really fits the form. However, if you are planning an object that has a purely decorative function, such as a wall hanging, you will discover that its actual shape can be modified so that it becomes part of the design.

While developing design ideas for the craft medium you enjoy, you will naturally want to explore the range of its possibilities to the utmost. Working with the materials of your medium is one of the greatest pleasures you can have as you come to really know your craft. The potter's clay may sometimes seem to have a will of its own. The qualities of materials play a major part in the type of design you will want to create. For best results, the physical components of a craft medium should not be forced into completely unnatural attitudes. They should be allowed to remain expressive of themselves. Wood is a beautiful substance in itself, with its grain, patina and inner glow. Since each material has its own integrity that should be respected, there would be little point in trying to make a carved wooden sculpture simulate one carved in stone. If you prefer stone sculpture, marble would be a more logical choice.

And so it is with all media—the basic qualities of the materials should not be overlooked or forgotten. As you plan a design, keep the particular strengths, weaknesses and other characteristics of your materials in mind.

It is possible to adapt similar design motifs to different areas of creativity. The favorite subject of one artist may be the same as that of another artist in an unrelated sphere, but the conception and carrying through of that idea may be entirely dissimilar. This is a natural occurrence. The flat forms of a two-dimensional work will not be the same as those needed in something with three dimensions, but they can often be based on the same subject matter.

This naturally raises the question of how to predict which types of design will work in your medium. The experience you have already gathered in handling your craft is an invaluable frame of reference. A minute detail that would be suitable to include as a single stitch in an embroidery would be completely lost in a shaggy loomed rug. As you are probably aware of this kind of limitation, you just have to think it over. The very shagginess of a rug can be incorporated to suggest a simpler outline or a bolder treatment of the chosen subject matter. There is really no subject that cannot be adapted.

You can learn to develop your sensitivity. Make yourself aware of the infinite variety of things that can influence your selection of materials and design inspiration. This includes a fresh look at the possibilities, as well as a knowledge of what has already been accomplished.

There is a constant interchange between all creative and productive processes. Just as art and architecture have been inextricably related throughout time, so are all manner of things. Designs are there to be seen when you know how to find them.

CHAPTER TWO

Design Basics

THE BASIC ELEMENTS OF DESIGN are like building blocks that can be used to create original plans for your own designs. They are the essential parts of every design and make up the general rules for assembling them together coherently.

The parts are the area, or space that the design will take place in, line, shape and form, color and texture. These are combined according to the principles of proportion, balance, emphasis, and rhythm.

When planning a design for a project, these concepts are applied so that it has a sense of oneness, the ideas of unity and harmony that are often referred to as a principle of design. It is a feeling that the parts are a whole, rather than a meaningless jumble. Once you have an understanding of these ideas, the groundwork for structuring your own designs is set. You can plan more easily with these helpful guidelines. Of course, the most careful following of these concepts will not always produce a great work of art, but they are quite useful in trying for a satisfying one.

Although you can probably make a design, and one that would please you, by using your familiarity with materials and your conceptualization of the end product, a working knowledge of the design basics will no doubt help you along. They are not hard to learn as they are based on well-founded logic that can be seen every day in paintings, architecture, fabrics and just about anything under the sun with a design.

SPACE

All designs take place in a certain amount of space. It's the working area of the design itself. Space, in most cases, is defined by a boundary, whether it is the outline of a vase or the edge of a piece of drawing paper. To visualize the space of your design, mark an area that will include the entire design, according to the article you want to make. The best thing to use is brown wrapping paper or large sheets of inexpensive drawing paper. Mark off the exact shape and size of the object planned. Then you will be able to see just how—and how much—the area needs to be worked. If necessary, tape sheets of paper together for a life-size model; that is most helpful, as a design made in the same proportions but on a smaller scale may not always be as effective when it is enlarged.

Within the boundaries of the now marked paper your design will take place. An important part of it is how the area is divided. A simple design motif may be placed in the center, or the space can be broken up into sections by the lines and shapes of the design. The organization of the shapes and lines can change the appearance of the space itself. For example, horizontal lines will make an area look wider than it is, while vertical lines will make it look taller. These are optical illusions that affect your perception of the area.

When using the space of a design, an essential feature is the use

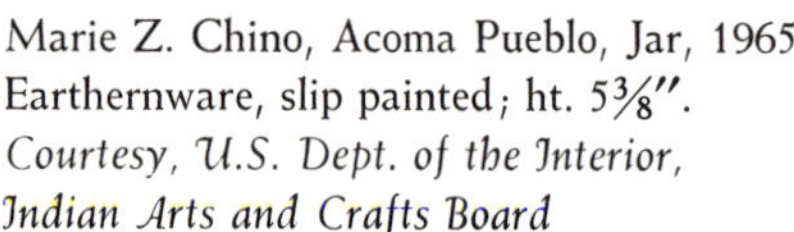

Marie Z. Chino, Acoma Pueblo, Jar, 1965. Earthernware, slip painted; ht. 5⅜″. *Courtesy, U.S. Dept. of the Interior, Indian Arts and Crafts Board*

of positive and negative space. The positive space is the actual shape and form of the design and the negative space is the background area that is not used or covered. The negative space remaining is just as important as the positive. If there is too little negative space, the design will seem overbearing or confused. If there is too much, your eye will have trouble following the design. The use of positive and negative space is most obvious when they are equal. This is often true of simple but effective black and white patterns, where each section is divided in a geometric pattern defined by similar areas of black and white.

In general, the division of space should be done so that the shapes within it are easily viewed as a whole. If you want the individual shapes to be perceived as independent units within the whole, there should be more space left around the objects than there is enclosed within a single shape or form. To make the shapes more of an entity, there should be less negative space allowed. This will make them seem more unified.

The two-dimensional quality of space on paper can be further altered by other optical illusions. If you overlap figures in a space, the one closest to the bottom, or the one shown most fully will appear to be in front, or closer to the viewer. This is also true of a series of overlapping shapes that decrease in size. Those that are smaller will appear to be farther away.

Overlapping figures in space. *Photo by Scott Chase Parker*

Perspective is shown by the converging lines of the poles and dock

The relative size of the shapes in relation to the space creates other illusions. If you place one shape near the lower front of the area, it will seem closer, and if it is near the top, farther away. However, if two identical shapes are placed together, the entire area seems to come forward.

To create a feeling of depth, the space is often divided so that the larger objects in the design are near the center or bottom and smaller ones near the top or around the central figure.

The idea of mechanical perspective as rediscovered and utilized in the fifteenth century is the effective means of achieving a feeling of depth. It is most commonly seen as a vanishing point, real or implied. If you see a river, a road or other similar depiction of a natural scene, their more or less parallel lines seem to converge as they move back, away from the viewer. As the river, for example, grows narrower toward the back of the picture, it seems to disappear, strengthening the illusion of distance.

LINE

Just about everything that is drawn starts with a line. Lines are used on their own or to define areas, shapes or forms. The concept of line is an artistic means of expressing something that exists in nature as merely the separation between one thing and the next. We are so used to the idea of lines that we see them everywhere.

Lines can be made in many ways. Lines can curve, go straight or blend together. To express movement, a vertical or diagonal line seems to draw your eye across the page. A sharper zigzagging line expresses more frenetic motion. A graceful, scalloped line seems more restful, although it still has movement. A plain horizontal line suggests repose, perhaps as it is the attitude of sleep and calm seas. A bold heavy line can seem like a shape—and who is to say it is not?

In design, line can be the only element, within a space. In calligraphy, this is true. The careful qualities of line used to form letters and sometimes forms is all there is. Oriental artists are renowned for

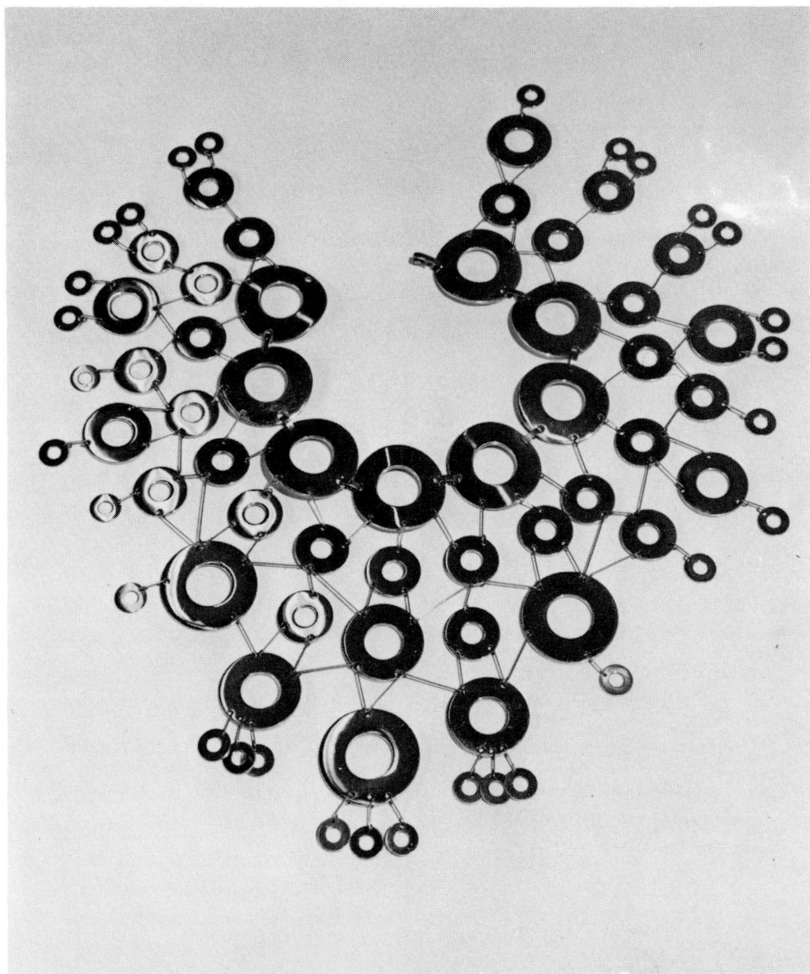

Mary Ann Scherr, "Circles and Lines". Stainless steel necklace. *Courtesy, Artist*

Above, Pile Cloth, Zaire: Kuba; Grasscloth, 138¼″ x 73¼″. *Courtesy of the Museum of Primitive Art, New York*

Left, Oil Drip Plate, Japan Edo Period, 18th-19th C. Seto. Diam. 9¾″. Orchids and Dragonfly design. *Seattle Art Museum, Eugene Fuller Collection. Courtesy, The Asia Society*

Line and direction in a random natural composition

their expressive use of line and their signatures on fine line paintings are calligraphic as well.

Lines also have an emotional aspect. They can be weak or strong, soft or hard, expressing different shades of feeling. To depict something as strong and sturdy, a thick smooth line is used. A thin wavering line makes an object appear weaker. Soft, fuzzy lines are often used to make things seem farther away, as they are clouded by the atmosphere in real life.

Another interesting quality of line is the eye's desire to fill in the gaps. If you draw a round line, left open at one point, your eye will appear to fill it in and it will be seen as a circle.

In the artistic use of line, the method of shading known as cross hatching is effective because our eyes fill in and blend the group of small black lines into a grey mass. This adds visual weight and substance to the shaded object.

The actual tools you use to make lines also change their characteristics. A brush and ink will give you an entirely different feeling

When a foreground object is the focal point, the background blurs with distance

than would a sharp pencil. Experiments with lines can include all kinds of media—pastels; oil or acrylic paints; charcoal; felt tip markers in thin and thick widths; soft and hard lead pencils; or crayons and water colors. See how each produces a certain kind of line and just what it is that makes them look so different. The way the paper absorbs the applied pigment is also variable. Draw lines on many types of paper to see how they change. Absorbent newsprint, bristol board with its slightly pebbly surface, the slickness of magazine stock, will all give you different sorts of lines.

SHAPE AND FORM

Shapes and forms are the objects created by lines or masses of color within a design area. In general, shapes are two dimensional and forms are three dimensional, or appear to be. As drawn on paper, both a square and a cube are technically two dimensional, but the cube has the illusion of three dimensionality.

Shapes and forms are thought of as geometric, realistic or abstract. Geometric shapes and forms are created with mathematical concepts and formulae. They are best drawn with specific instruments like compasses when their qualities are meant to be precise. Geometric shapes and forms are further separated from each other by the use of

Form and shape

Sally Lee Begay, Navajo, Rug. 1963. Wool; 57¼" x 60". *Courtesy, U.S. Dept. of the Interior, Indian Arts and Crafts Board*

perspective and shading. When you add the illusion of the third dimension, it can be strengthened by shading placed to emulate the reaction of light falling upon the form.

Realistic forms or shapes are drawn to represent nature by depicting an actual object, somewhat as a photograph would. They are often referred to as representational since you know right away what the object is. This is also enhanced by shading to add weight and mass to the object shown.

Abstract forms are an impression of natural form rendered in a simpler or otherwise changed way. Often we can discern what is being shown, but it will have a more emotional or individual quality. Other shapes known as free form or biomorphic can be said to fall

Necklace, Ghana: Ashanti, Gold, 15¼″ long. *Courtesy of the Museum of Primitive Art, New York*

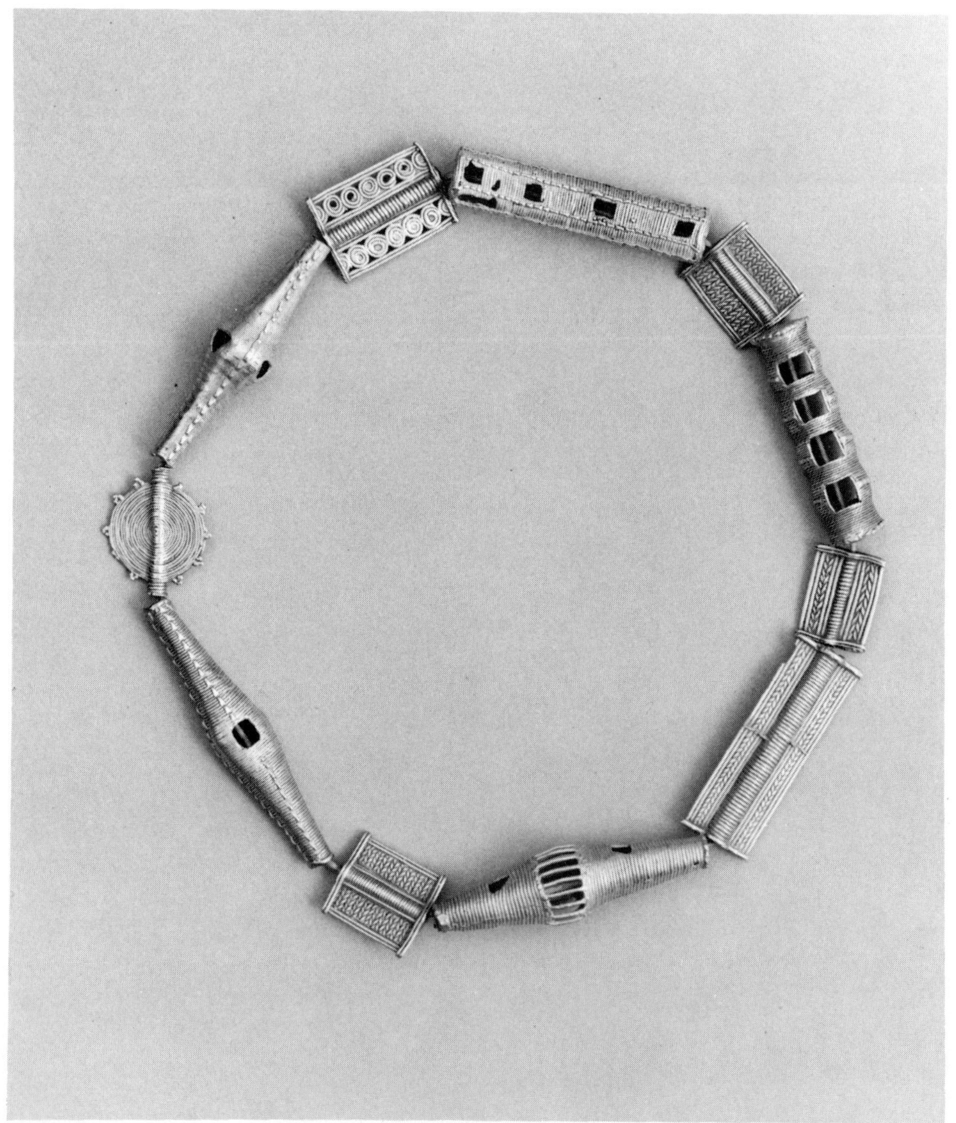

Bird, Japan, Edo Period, ht. 11″. Wood. *Collection of Mr. and Mrs. Myron S. Falk, Jr., New York City. Courtesy, The Asia Society*

Textile Fragment, Peru, wool and cotton, ht. 24½″. *Courtesy of the Museum of Primitive Art, New York*

within the realm of abstractions, as you can abstract a natural form to the point where it is unrecognizable. Free forms in the strictest sense are non-objective or designed to represent nothing but themselves. These shapes can be drawn at will or adapted from the shape suggestion of an unrelated article.

When you want to add realism or weight to a design, the forms and shapes you use are most important. They should be chosen and manipulated in the way that seems most natural. The study of actual objects is helpful, and you should take particular note of how light

Stone free form

falls on the object, where the shadows are, where highlights might be suggested, and how a feeling of weight seems to be created.

(Color and texture are discussed in their own chapters.)

THE PRINCIPLES OF DESIGN

When you put all the shapes, forms, lines, colors and textures together in the space of a design, you combine them according to the concepts of proportion, balance, emphasis and rhythm in the hope of creating harmony or unity. These ideas are referred to as the principles of design. They are applied to the working methods of placement and visualization of the elements of design.

These principles are intended to help you in creating a plan that can be followed. The plan, or design, is a unit. It should be such that all of the parts work together to form a satisfying whole. No one element should be overwhelming or discordant. On the other hand, the design should not be so unified as to appear repetitious. Variety adds the note of interest that changes a design to make it more individual and exciting.

PROPORTION

Proportion is the use of shapes and sizes that relate well to each other and to the whole. They are arranged in space so that they harmonize in terms of the entire unit. Proportion is often a matter of ratio. In ancient Greece, the Golden Oblong rule of proportion was the use of a ratio of 1 to 1.618. It was applied to architecture and drawing with pleasing results. Of course, not all things should be proportioned this way, but it is interesting to see how well it works.

The scale, or relationship of sizes in design elements is often based on realistic interpretation. This is the lifelike juxtaposition of articles so that they are in the same scale, or relation of size to each other as they really are. We know that a flower is smaller than a tree and it usually looks best that way. The same may be true for any realistic grouping, unless a particular segment is exaggerated for design purposes. In geometric or free form designs, the proportion is totally dependent on the visual relationship of the parts. They are sized to balance each other in a pleasing way.

In using proportion, the sizes can go well together in terms of their

similarity. They should be unlike enough to be interesting, yet not so unlike as to seem disconnected.

In short, proportion is needed to create a design that is satisfying in its spatial relationships. The scale of the forms, the division of space and the good use of the parts to the whole are essential.

When dealing with proportion, assemble the parts of the design. Then you can experiment with them to discover proportions that are pleasing to you. Make small sketches, trying out small, medium and large shapes and forms. Test the relationship of the various elements. You can change the ones that seem too large or too small so that they work together. Especially in geometric and free form patterns you can adapt the parts until they seem just right.

BALANCE

To balance a design, you place the shapes and forms within it so that they create an illusion of equal tensions, or visual weights. As each segment has this quality of eye tension or weight, they are balanced so that neither side is uneven in weight or distracting. Your eye will perceive a well-balanced design as a feeling of completeness.

The idea of balance can be most easily thought of as in an old-fashioned scale, where the two sides actually balance against each other. The mass can balance the other side without being the same size, as would the proverbial pound of feathers and pound of iron.

The most widely used form of balance of a classical nature is formal balance, where each side of the design is the same. In this type of balance, also known as symmetrical for obvious reasons, each half of

Left, Embroidered panel by the Battye Family to William Morris & Co. design. *Courtesy, William Morris Gallery*

Right, Kay Whitcomb, "Tree", Bread Ornament, 14″ x 11″. *Courtesy, Artist*

Carved wooden bookends

the design on the left and right is equally spaced and more or less identical and therefore automatically balanced. This creates a static image that seems passive, with little motion involved.

Balance is created when the sides are not identical by the use of equal distances and sizes. The balance can then be symmetrical in the sense that the parts have equal tensions and are the same distance apart.

Informal, or asymmetrical balance uses different types or sizes of form and division of space. They are balanced forming an illusion of having equal tensions due to other characteristics. This type of balance is also called dynamic, active or occult, because there is a feeling of movement and vigor achieved. It is a more difficult balance to work with than the quieter formal balance, but good results are stimulating and interesting to look at.

In balance, the size and color, as well as the number and type of shapes you use affect the design. Since it is an illusion of equal weight there are many optical qualities that come into play. Dark colors or larger forms appear to be heavier than lighter or smaller ones. Again, think of a scale, or a mobile. The actual weight of the objects in a mobile create its balance and are the determining factor. In informal balance, the impression given by the design elements are what does it. A single large or heavy looking shape on one side can be balanced by two or more smaller, or lighter looking shapes in opposition.

The placement of forms and shapes affects the balance. A small bright shape near the top of a design can unbalance it by drawing your eye up and out of the picture. The colors are important in that dark, warm or bright colors tend to add weight to a shape, while the light values and cool colors seem lighter in weight as well.

Balance is a means of obtaining a feeling of repose. Here again,

Informal balance in nature

experimentation is a must. Cut out paper shapes so that they can be moved around, until they seem to be equal in tension. Try out various schemes until one seems best. Informal balance is more lively, while formal balance can create a classic look.

Above, The small bright form of the frog balances the mass of the cannon. *Photo by Olga Ley*

Right, McBride Lomayestewa, Hopi Pueblo, Plaque, 1966. Yucca, coiled; 14⅝″. *Courtesy, U.S. Dept. of the Interior, Indian Arts and Crafts Board*

EMPHASIS

Emphasis is the concept that there is always a center of interest or a dominant part of every design. This is not the actual center, although it may be. It is more a point where your eye is inevitably drawn as you look at the design. You see it first, then the surrounding parts. These are called the subordinates as they serve to bring your eye back to the dominant feature. They can be thought of as lesser points of interest. Subordinates are essential to a design as they will keep your eye moving within the design, rather than allowing it to move out and away from it, due to a distracting influence. The emphasis is working well when your eye follows a path from point to point without ever leaving the picture. When it is uneven, your eye wanders aimlessly, without a central unification by dominance or an organizing technique.

The parts that are emphasized draw your attention in many ways.

Bobbi Beck, "Party"

The placement, spacing, color, brightness and intensity, texture and pattern of the design elements all contribute. In the art world, the use of unseen underlying geometric eye plans are used for emphasis. In Da Vinci's *Last Supper* the entire fresco is structured on a series of giant triangles that always bring your eye back to the central figure.

These techniques can be used to create an emphasis that really allows you to look at a design without confusion. In general, the central figure of a design is placed within the realm of the actual center, or a bit to the left or right. Then the subordinate elements are structured around it.

RHYTHM

Rhythm is the sense of movement within a design. It is created by the pattern your eye follows along the path of interest. As such, it is strongly related to emphasis. The rhythm can be fast or slow, like the rhythm in music. It is the feeling generated by the eye as it perceives the design. What counts here is that your eye moves well and easily, whatever type of rhythm is used.

There are several methods of creating a satisfying rhythm so that the stress or accent falls on the appropriate parts of the design. Gradation or progression of shapes and related line within the design create rhythm as they gradually grow larger or smaller. Similarly, repetition of a particular shape produces interesting rhythm as long as there is variety as well.

The use of repetition in a different way for rhythm is the basis of the repeat type of pattern found in fabrics and wall paper. This is a design or pattern where a central motif, often composed of several forms, is planned so that successive printings produce an all-over unified pattern. The sides, top and bottom of the central section are carefully worked so that they fit together perfectly to form a continuous design.

The spacing and changes in color intensity or texture can also affect the rhythm. If you look at a design with several separate bright spots, your eye will move quickly over the surface and a feeling of motion will be generated. If you look at another design with a series of related undulating wave shapes, the feeling will be more peaceful and quiet, like the tranquil ripples on a pond.

HARMONY AND UNITY

When you see a design that seems just right and holds together in one integral unit, it has achieved a sense of unity. This is often thought of as the last design principle. It is the whole point—to make your design a well-organized, integrated unit with a pleasant sense of harmony.

Banner, Japan, Edo Period, 106″ x 15½″. Hemp fiber painted with tiger design and family crest. *Collection, Japan Society, New York. Courtesy, The Asia Society*

Left, Kay Whitcomb, "View from the Moon", Enamel on Steel, 20″ x 30″, made at Gustavsberg, Sweden, and bought the day of the first moon walk. *Collection of Mr. and Mrs. Jacob Bronowski. Courtesy, Artist*

Right, Planning a repeat unit for a fabric design by Nancy Greenberg and the author.

This is an ineffable quality that occurs after time and experimentation. You can understand the concept better by studying the works of well known artists since this principle is shared and often well expressed in painting. It is a matter of seeing many examples of works that made use of all these principles to their best advantages. You will soon come to recognize and utilize them in your own work. Keep in mind the often quoted thought that an artist works for order and hopes for beauty.

"Rose and Lily", Silk and Wool, designed by William Morris. *Courtesy, William Morris Gallery*

CHAPTER THREE

The Importance Of Color

ONE OF THE FIRST THINGS that strikes the eye when one looks at a good design is the use of color. Color can be crucial to the end result because good color selection can make an otherwise plain design appear more interesting and alive. On the other hand, an unfortunate combination of colors can make an exciting design dull and ineffective.

When a beam of light passes through a prism, it is broken up into the individual wave lengths of colored light, namely, red, orange, yellow, green, blue, indigo and violet. These are the colors of a rainbow, which is produced in nature when light passes through droplets of water. The wave lengths of light are what enable us to perceive color. When light falls on a colored object, the light is partially absorbed by the object and only the waves of its color are reflected back to the eye. If the object is red, then all of the wave lengths are absorbed with the exception of the red ones, which are reflected and perceived as the sensation of the color red.

Another quality of light is that it can be transmitted as well as absorbed or reflected. This occurs when the object is not solid, but translucent, like colored glass. A red glass absorbs all but the red light which is transmitted so that everything seen through the glass appears to be red.

Light is pure so that when all of the wave lengths are blended, the composite result is white light. In the case of pigments or other mediums used by artists, the blending of all the colors produces gray.

The basic colors used in light study, known as the primary colors, are generally thought of as red, green and blue-purple. They combine to yield white light when mixed in the right proportions and are known as additive colors. They will make up the greatest number of different colors when added to each other and that is why they are primary.

When using paints or other pigments, there are several color theories that can be considered. The one most widely used has red, yellow and blue as the primary colors. They can be combined to make up the largest amount of different colors, but no mixture of the other colors will produce red, yellow or blue.

In this theory, a color wheel is used to express the relationship between colors. The primary colors are spaced at equal distances around the circle or wheel so that an equilateral triangle can be drawn to connect them within the wheel. The secondary colors are spaced at equal distances between the primaries, depicting their relationship as the result of mixtures of the two primary colors they fall between. The secondary colors are orange, green and violet.

A third group of colors, known as tertiary, are placed on the wheel between a primary and the closest secondary color and are a result of

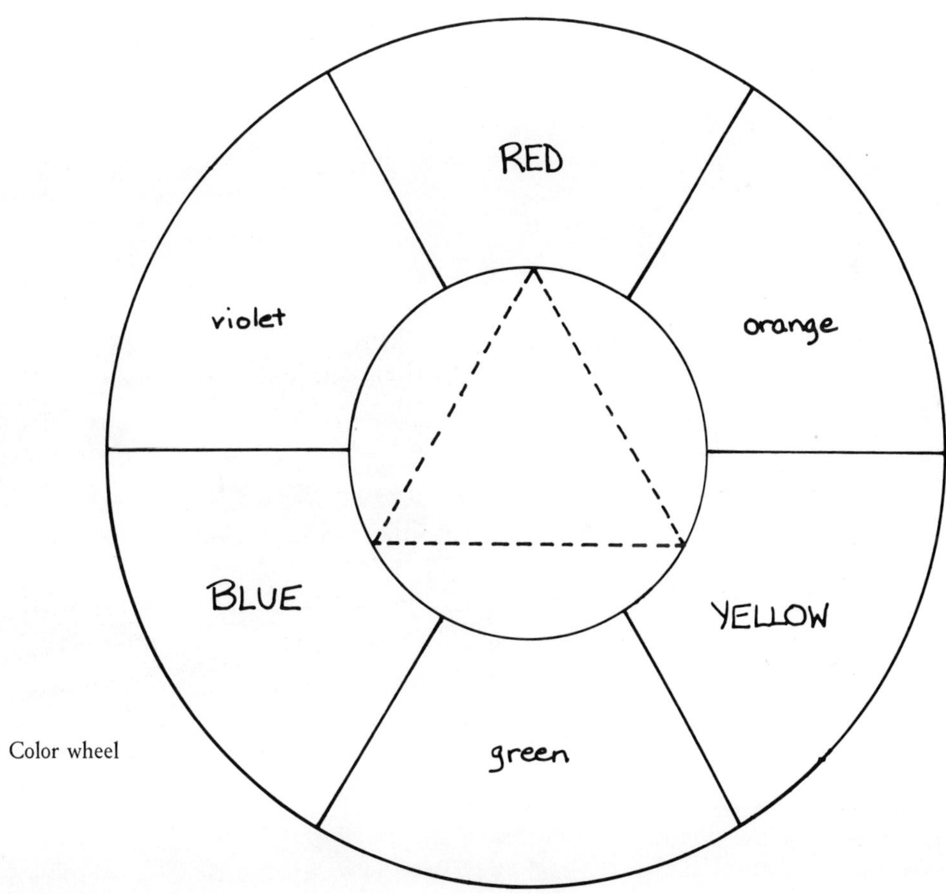

Color wheel

their mixture. The tertiary colors are red-orange, yellow-orange, yellow-green, blue-violet and red violet.

The pure colors of pigment are called normal hues. The normal hues that are included most often in actual work are referred to as standard hues. These are the primary and secondary colors, red, orange, yellow, green, blue and violet.

When we use these colors they are thought of as complementary in certain relationships. The complementary colors are found opposite each other on the color wheel and are red and green, yellow and violet, blue and orange. When the complementary colors are placed next to each other in a composition, they strengthen and brighten each other. If they are mixed together in the same intensity, they form gray, due to the fact that they include all of the colors on the wheel in their mixture.

Hue is the name or family of a color. When referring to the normal hue, it is the pure color of pigments. Intensity, or chroma, is the brightness, saturation, or amount of gray in a color. The normal hue is the most intense or brilliant form of a color, with no gray in it. To change the intensity of a normal hue, you add its complement or gray, black, or white. This will dull the intensity regardless of which one you add.

The value of a color is its lightness or darkness. The value is expressed on terms of steps in progression from black to white. It is said that the average eye can distinguish seven grays in this progression

This page, Margaret Sussman, silver and enamel box. *Photo by Erich Vogel. Courtesy, Artist*

Opposite, Blackthorn wallpaper designed by William Morris. *Courtesy, William Morris Gallery*

Above, Futon Cover, Japan, Edo Period, 60¾″ x 48½″, Cotton, "mattress" cover with dyed Paulownia and Phoenix Design. *Collection, Japan Society, New York. Courtesy, The Asia Society*

and for that reason these are the most widely used. You may have been surprised to see a black and white photograph of three different colored objects that all looked the same shade of gray in the picture. This happens when the values of the colors were the same even though the colors of the objects themselves were different. In order to raise or lighten the value, it is necessary to add white. To lower or darken the value, add black. In terms of value, the colors will reach a point where they become white or black at the extremes because no hue can accommodate that light or dark a value. When referring to values, the terms tint and shade are used. A tint is a value above the normal hue for a specific color while a shade is a value below the normal hue for that color. The distinction is made because each normal color has its own value. For example, the normal value of blue is always darker than the normal value of yellow. Pastels are light values of any color with gray added.

If you mix gray with a hue, the result is a tone. There are actually as many tones possible as there are grays in the value scale. These also end just before reaching white or black in either direction.

Whenever you add a complement to a color in order to dull the intensity, the value will change as well. To add the complement for lesser intensity without lowering or darkening the value, add some white as well at the same time.

Our perception of color greatly affects its characteristics. Colors are thought of as cool or warm. The cool colors are blue, green, violet, and all the combinations thereof. [They are the colors of the sky, the night, and water—all cool.] The warm colors are red, yellow, and orange—the colors of earth, sun, clay and sand. The cool colors are thought of as restful and quiet while the warm colors are livelier. There is some question as to the status of violet, which has red in it, but for the most part it is thought of as cool.

The cool colors have the optical effect of appearing to recede in space so that a blue wall would seem further away than a brown one. The warm colors seem closer and larger in size. This is important to the image you want to create and convey. The warm colors also have the effect of unifying shapes and forms placed on them as a background. The cooler colors somehow seem to pull apart the other colors placed on them and separate the shapes or forms into more independent units.

You should also keep in mind the fact that texture affects color. A rough surface naturally absorbs more light than a smooth one even if they are identical in color. Rough surfaces will also appear less brilliant in color than smooth or shiny ones.

Another interesting effect created by our perception of color is illustrated by the grouping of dots or small bands of color. This effective technique can be seen in the pointillist paintings by Seurat. As you look at what is known as the broken colors, your eye tends to blend them together so that dots of blue and yellow actually appear green. The resultant color as blended by your eye somehow seems more brilliant and shimmering than a thoroughly mixed color of the same shade. This feeling can be achieved in mixed wools or the tesserae of mosaics.

When it comes right down to choosing a color scheme for your work, there are many options open to you. Traditional color schemes can be utilized with interesting results. Or you may prefer to make a personal statement in a new and different choice of colors that seem just right for what you have in mind. All colors are versatile and attractive in that no one can really say that one combination or another that appeals to you is bad. They might not like the results on a personal basis, but that is something else again.

One of the most valuable aids in selecting your color schemes is a set of water color paints. You can use them to experiment with various plans and you will certainly have fun just blending the various colors to see the outcome. A child's paintbox with the six widely used standard colors is sufficient to begin with and can produce colors you will want. Black and white will also be helpful as an additional change in values. As you combine and explore the colors, look carefully at each one. Notice how little gray it takes to change the values, then try out the effects of black and white. The more you are able to distinguish small variations, the more effective will be your use of color.

A complementary color scheme is one that uses one color and its complement. As these have no mixed color in common, they tend to compete with each other for attention and will seem quite bright. This is most true when the colors are at normal value. For added variation, use a less intense value of either color by adding a bit of the other. You can also try out many more schemes by changing each color as much as possible while sticking to the two hues.

A monochromatic scheme, as the name implies, is one where one color is used. All of the shades, tints and tones which can be made in the hue are included. Just think of all the different color greens there are in the world and you will appreciate the possibilities of this type of grouping.

An analogous color scheme is made by selecting colors that appear next to each other on the color wheel. These colors just naturally seem to go together because they share a color in common. For example, in the use of violet, blue-violet, and blue. You can expand the analogous scheme in this case by adding blue-green and green and for more variety, by including the five colors that have blue in common.

Another kind of scheme is created by choosing a group of colors and adding a single color to all of them. The single color will serve to unify the others by adding something that they all have in common. This produces related colors in that if you add a touch of red to any three or more choices, they will all be related through the red even though they are otherwise different.

Triadic color schemes are achieved by using three colors that are equally spaced on the wheel. These will be lively combinations in themselves due to their three basically different color ingredients, as in the choice of orange, violet and green for example. If you prefer a more subtle triadic combination, add a little black, white or gray. The normal hues of orange, violet and green can be quickly transformed into pale apricot, lavender and light green with the addition of white and gray, and that is only one of the variations possible. You may decide to select three colors and work with them alone. Even as such, the combinations you can produce through mixing and blending and experimentation are one of the real pleasures of working with color, and the experience is worth having.

The neutrals play an important part in color schemes. Black used as a background will make colors appear brighter than they actually are. Pale gray or white have the effect of darkening their foreground colors. Beige, which is an extremely light value of brown with gray in it, is a good neutral kind of color to work with as a background due to its warmish quality and unifying effect. You can start with a brown base by mixing black, orange, red and a drop of green. Add white and a touch of gray as needed for the beige you have in mind.

The idea of dominance, subordination and accent is applied to a color scheme when you choose a moderately bland color as your dominant one, a slightly brighter color for the second support and a much brighter color in small amounts for accent. This is used frequently in the traditional decorating idea of a neutral or beige for major pieces in a room, such as walls and rugs, with two lesser amounts of other colors for contrast and accent.

Observe the use of color in the articles around you. Look at a fabric or wall paper that appeals to you. In most cases you will find that what you liked about the object the most and what attracted you to it in the first place was the use of color. Is one outstanding? Are the largest areas bright or dull? Are the smaller parts of the pattern noticeable because of their hue? What properties do the colors have in relationship to each other? If you ask yourself these questions each time you encounter a pleasing use of color, you will soon develop the ability to recognize the components that make the object appealing to you. Study the color make-up of familiar things; boxes of consumer goods, a well-put-together room, the latest fashion—see what is being done. Whenever possible, save a small sample of anything with colors that you find especially attractive. Save these bits and pieces and consult them for new ideas. They will help you formulate original concepts by providing examples that have been used effectively elsewhere.

Look for the natural color schemes that exist in life itself. Nature is said to be the master of form and it can be added that it is the master of color as well. Only a master artist could successfully combine all the colors that make up a butterfly's wing for such a breathtaking result. The deep blue of a near night sky over snow-capped purple mountains not only suggests a great color scheme, but is a design inspiration as well.

The emotional aspects of color are well known. Everyone knows what it means to be feeling blue. When we are angry, we see red. These are all real reactions that can occur and can be important in planning the aspects of color in design. The many colorful expressions are indicative of the possibilities of using color to create a mood.

What you are planning to make is another influence on the colors you will want to choose. If you are creating an art work to hang in the living room, it is logical to take the colors already in the room into consideration. Not only will you find that the colors of your furnishings have an impact on the things that will go well with them, but you can be reasonably sure that the colors surrounding you are ones that you feel comfortable living with.

When you are planning to make a gift for someone you know, think of the colors they like to wear, or the scheme of their home furnishings. Then you will be able to choose colors they will like just by careful observation.

If you plan to sell your work, you might make use of the hues that are currently in fashion. These are easily found in magazines and the model rooms of fine department stores. Of course, the ultimate choice will be tempered by your own taste and good judgment.

Another major consideration is what your work will be used for. If you are making a set of stoneware plates, remember that they will not only have to look well in themselves, but will also have food on them. This principle is used to advantage by butchers who often display meat with parsley on or near it. As the complement of red, the green leaves make meat look brighter and more inviting. For any type of functional work, this type of thought should be included. Just envision the object in use for a better idea of how the colors will work.

Color is so challenging that it can became a real mark of distinction. With experimentation and observation, you will plan color schemes as original and exciting as your work.

CHAPTER FOUR

Texture

WHEN DESIGNING FOR A CRAFT MEDIUM, one of the foremost considerations is the texture and nature of the materials used. Each type of work has its own characteristics and texture; this is undoubtedly one of the reasons why someone particularly enjoys a certain area of expression. Handling and seeing the many textures is so much a part of one's reactions that it might help explain why one person prefers weaving or embroidery, with soft fuzzy wools and tough fibers, while another prefers the smooth glazes of ceramics or the hard beauty of opalescent glasses in leaded windows.

Texture is both visual and tactile. You can appreciate the velvety pile of a rug without actually touching it. On the other hand, you can create a textural appearance on a basically non-textured surface.

The sense of touch is so important to our orientation that we learn early on what something will—or ought to—feel like without touching it. The surfaces of many objects are likely to trigger an emotional response. Long after childhood we may still feel comforted by the plushy surface of a stuffed toy, without even being conscious of it. The fluffy fur of a cat or the hard crisp quality of a dog's hair are ones we have grown accustomed to liking.

When we speak of texture in the visual sense, we mean the image reflected back to our minds by the surface of an object. The visual impression is created by the various planes or surfaces of the material and the way in which they respond to light. Surfaces absorb and re-

Right, June Schwarcz, electroplated foil, diam. 6½″, ht. 4½″. *Courtesy, Artist*

Paul Ratajczak. *Photo by Michael Paulin*

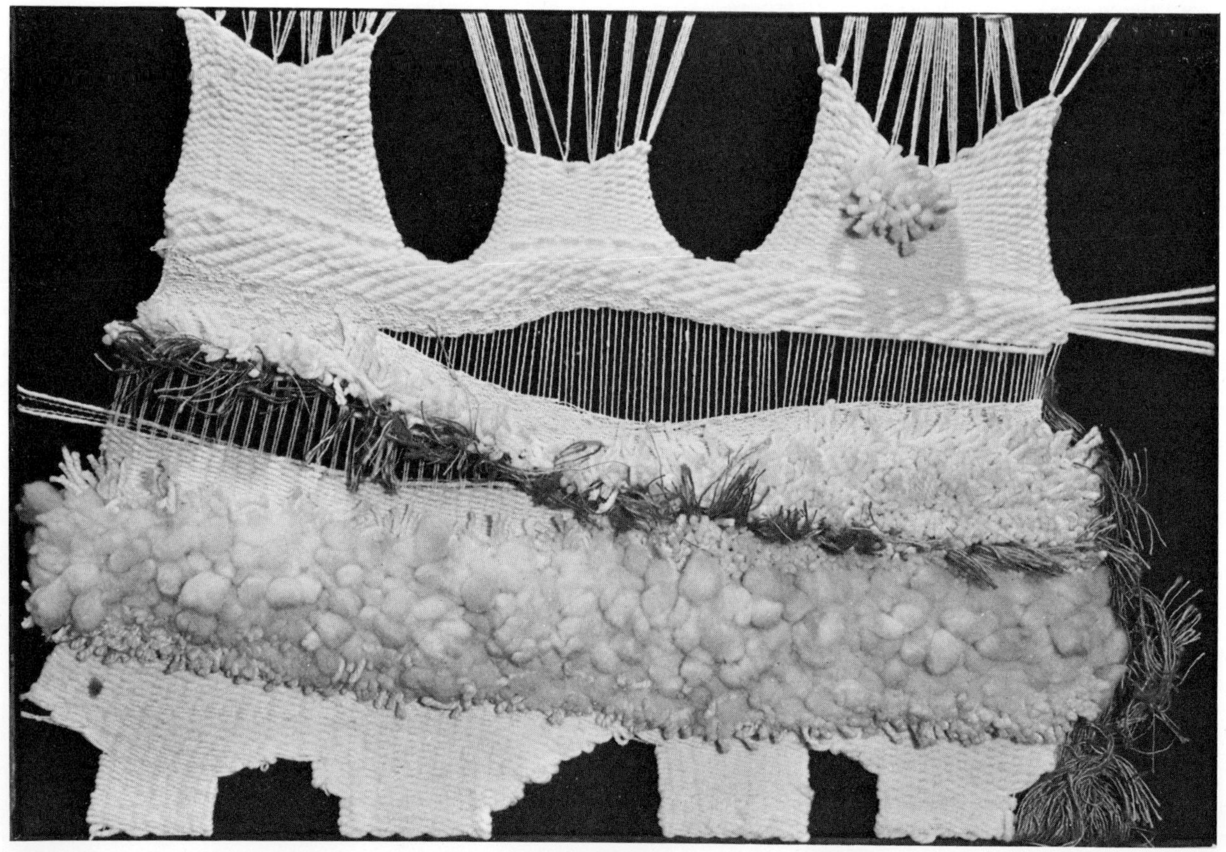

flect light to varying degrees and we perceive these differences as texture.

Depending upon how an object receives the light striking it, we refer to its surface qualities as opaque, translucent or transparent.

An opaque object seems impenetrable by light, reflecting an image of solid color and texture. If the opaque surface is broken up into many planes, it appears rougher than one with a more uniform planed surface.

A translucent article will permit light to pass through it, becoming diffused on the way. This gives you the feeling of luminescence, while you cannot actually see objects on the other side. This is often true of fine bone china, which will allow light to pass through it in a diffused way and is often used as a minor test of its quality.

A transparent object is one that transmits light to the extent that you can see through it, like a pane of glass. If the transparent object

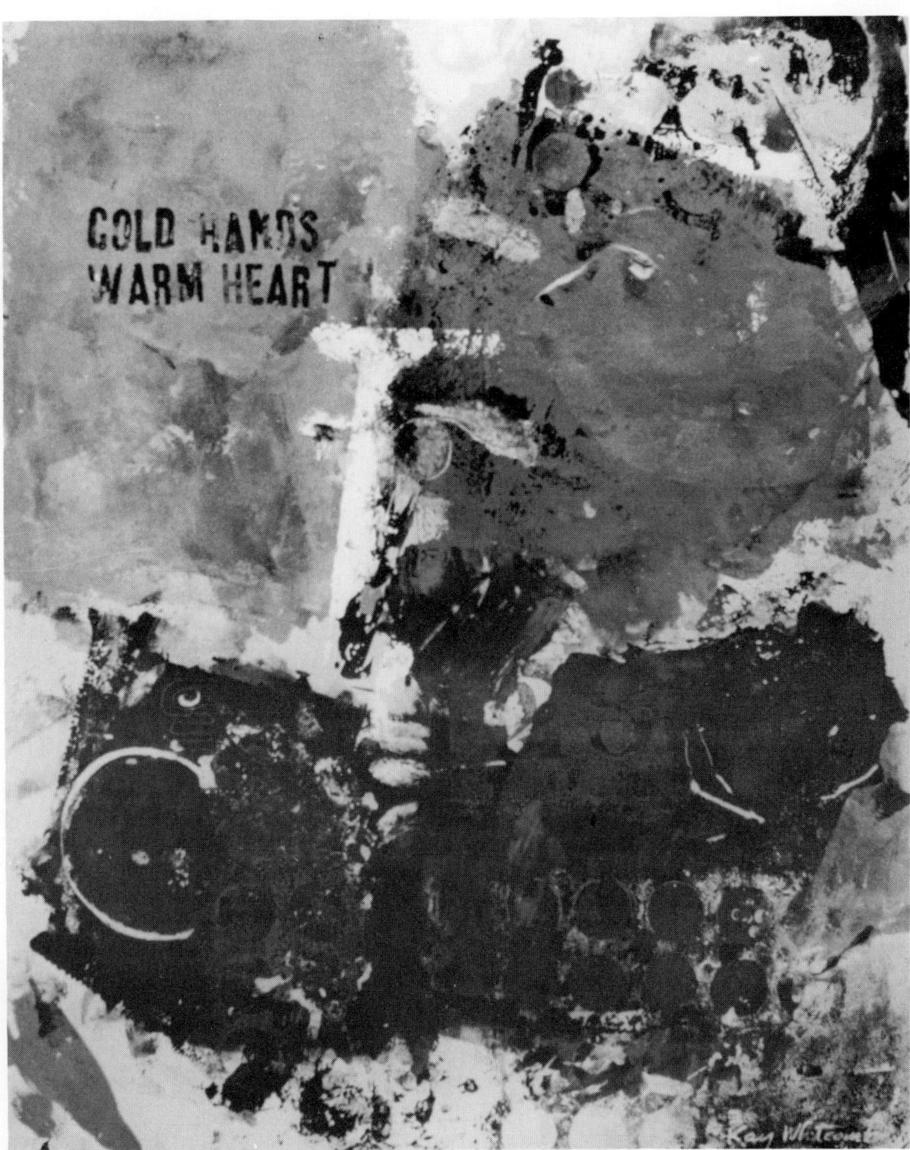

Kay Whitcomb, "Cold Hands, Warm Heart", Enamel on Steel, 14″ x 18″, 1971. Made at Crahait Factory, Belgium.
Courtesy, Artist

Bronze horse

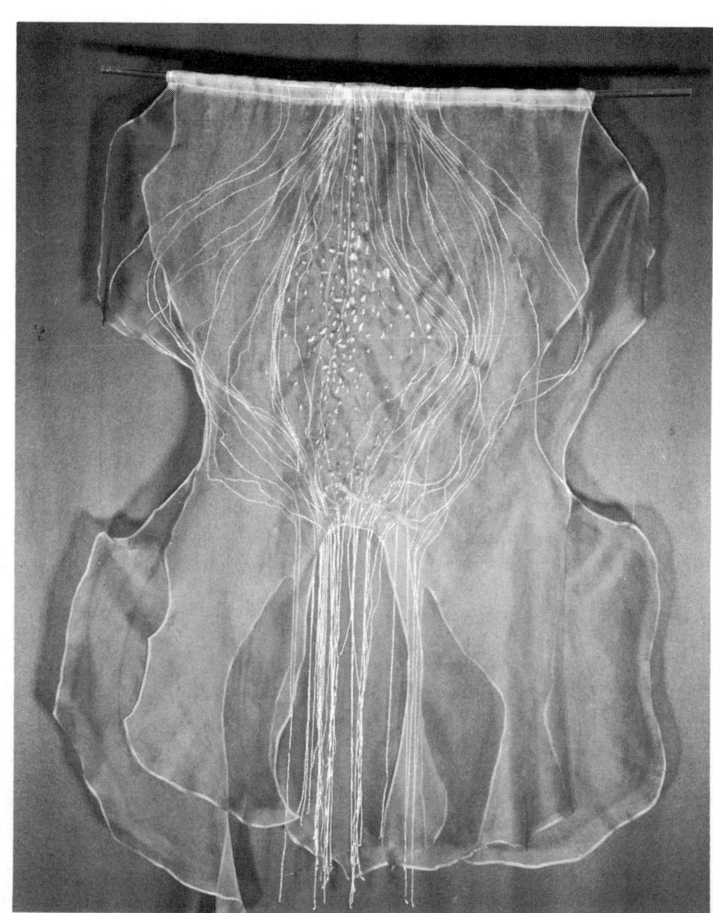

Kiyomi Iwata, Chiffon, White on White

Tom McGlaughlin.
Courtesy, Artist

has its own color, everything seen through it will appear to be that color. And truly transparent substances, such as clear glass and water, are the only things that exist without a color of their own.

The tactile qualities of texture make us think of things as hard or soft, rough or smooth. These characteristics also affect the perception of color, as rough surfaces absorb more light, appearing deeper and darker than highly polished surfaces of the same color.

An interesting experience is to gather a group of articles with various surface qualities. Include as many objects as you can find, among them objects made out of wood, ivory or bone, natural ores, crystals and geodes, stones and pebbles of different weights, sizes and shapes, porcelain, small ceramics of all sorts, feathers, worked metals in jewelry and so on. Hundreds of materials can be included. Cover your eyes and examine each article by feeling alone, deciding what it is, what it is made of and really getting to know it. Or, get a friend to join in and alternate turns so that you do not know what the object

Left, Mary Ann Scherr, Container Bracelet, Gold and Silver. *Courtesy, Artist*

Below, Margaret Sussman, Box 2½″, Silver with Rutile Quartz. *Photo by Erich Vogel. Courtesy, Artist*

Susie Billy, Pomo, Basket, ca. 1952. Coiled basket with feathers woven in, shell beads, 6″. *Courtesy, U.S. Dept. of the Interior, Indian Arts and Crafts Board*

is before you hold it in your hands. Another idea is to gather swatches of fabric in as many diverse fibers as possible and explore them the same way. The object is to enhance your sense of touch so that it really is sensitive. In almost all cases, you will know what you are holding, or will realize what it is in short order. However, to touch something without prior knowledge will increase your awareness of texture, because you are not influenced by color and other distractions.

As you develop a new sensitivity, you will find greater visual appreciation of textures. After handling and really enjoying a piece of ivory, the next time you see one that you cannot touch, you will savor both of its qualities.

Renie B. Adams, "Speckled Coffee Pot #2", Crocheted Cotton, ht. 8″. *Courtesy, Artist*

Although all surfaces have their own textures, you can increase the textural qualities of surfaces, like paper or canvas. Great artists of the Renaissance were so attuned to the lifelike depiction of texture that you can almost feel the heavily brocaded velvets and jewels on the clothing of people in portraits. Modern artists can create other textural effects with equal artistry, if not equal realism.

Try out the textures created by various artist's mediums, so that you understand them more thoroughly. Using oil paints or acrylics, try painting super smooth surfaces. Then dab on heavier blobs of paint for interesting raised areas. Vary the thickness of the paint itself with linseed oil or acrylic medium. See what the effects of more or less paint on the brush are on the surface you are working. For a

Basket weave terra cotta

fascinating textural effect, some artists use a thin flexible-bladed palette knife to spread paint on canvas.

Another textural experiment you may enjoy is painting with water colors. They can make soft muted shapes when applied to predampened paper. The same paint and brush on dry paper will give you different results. Paper with a pebbly surface will seem to pull the paint from the brush in a new way. Felt tip markers, pastels and pencils are also interesting to explore for new textural ideas.

Textural basket weave

Collage and montage are art forms that really lend themselves to textural experience. Collage is an assembling of cut or torn papers in various colors and types to create an abstract, textural composition, while montage generally includes photographs, prints or other figurative items as well. The distinction between the two is not always considered to be that significant and the term collage has come to include both techniques. The origins of collage are found in the art of Picasso and Braque who used the "papiers collés," or cut papers, in new ways as a Cubist form of expression near the turn of this century.

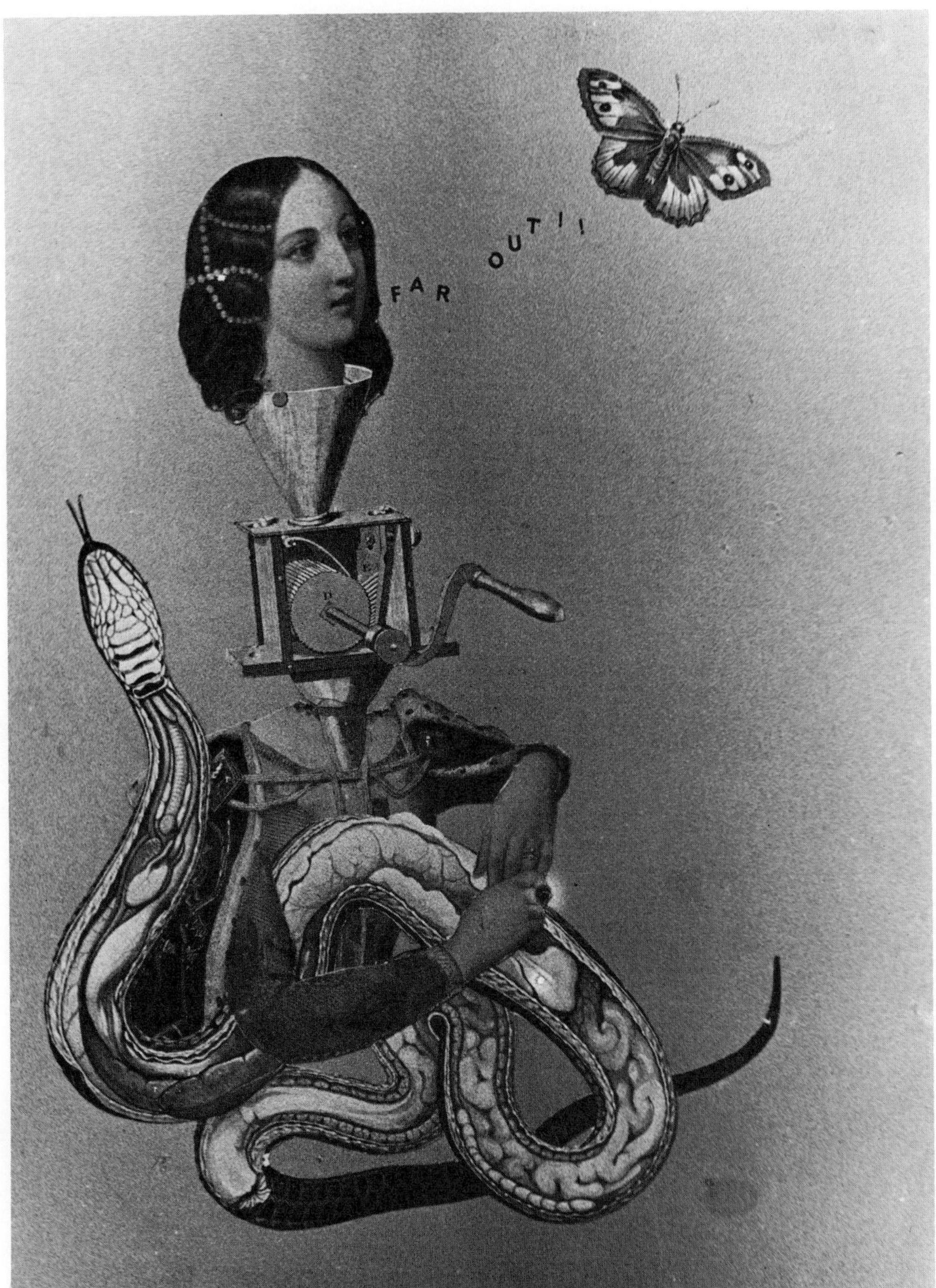

Joan Hall, "Collage 2". *Courtesy, Artist*

You will find that there is a lot of fun in working with these techniques. You can include different paper materials such as newsprint, photographs, magazines, cardboard, construction paper, colored tissue paper, wrapping paper, brightly colored Japanese Origami papers and drawing paper. The simplest bits and scraps of paper can be used, moving them around as much as you like before pasting them down. This is also a good way to explore abstract design, using the colors you prefer, or those you want to try in new combinations. Cut or tear free forms, using tissue paper in layers for translucent effects, or construction paper for heavier, more solid forms. Assemble them as they look most exciting to you.

For more expressive, figurative collage, you can use printed gift wrapping papers, playing and greeting cards, Victorian valentines, paper doilies, wall paper, or in short just about anything you can cut up and paste down. The flexibility of this technique produces fascinating results. And when finished, you will not only have a wealth of design and textural inspiration, but also a work that will probably be of such interest on its own that you will want to hang it on your wall.

A further technique for creating visual textures is to make a frottage, or rubbing, as it was first developed by artist Max Ernst in the early 1900's. He was interested in the independent image created by objects in nature when covered by paper and rubbed with graphite. To try it out yourself, you can use medium weight paper and graphite or a soft blunt lead pencil. Cover a plank of wood, a bas relief carving or other textured surface with a piece of the paper. Then rub it lightly and carefully with the graphite or pencil so that the paper does not tear. The textural impression will appear on the paper. This creates a pattern with a style and life of its own.

This method is currently enjoying a resurgence as an art form, particularly in regard to making rubbings from the gravestones in old American churchyards, in a new appreciation of this type of folk art. It is also used in the study of such ancient cultures as the Mayans, who left many stellae, or monumental carved blocks of stone. By making rubbings, archaelogists and other students of these cultures can study the works without having to remove them from their original sites.

As you learn to use textural characteristics in various ways, you will find them of great help in planning designs for your work. As you formulate ideas, you will think of the tactile qualities of the craft medium and will know just how to use them to their best advantage.

If you make jewelry, you are aware of the different qualities of, for example, gold and copper, and know which to choose for the effect you desire to convey. And this type of knowledge is invaluable in all

Opposite, Mary Ann Scherr, Liquid crystal necklace with peacock feathers. Stainless steel and liquid crystals. 12½" x 8½". *Courtesy, Artist*

areas. As you need an understanding of the characteristics of materials, the textural sense is one of the major components. This is due to the fact that textural considerations can be most demanding. If you knit, you understand the lovely texture of angora and how difficult it is to take out a stitch if you make a mistake. Therefore, you will select it for a basic stitch and let the texture stand on its own to make the pattern. This sort of consideration points out the dependency of the effects you want on the materials you can select. If you find that

Weathered wood

Photos by Martin Last

Bark

Sand gulls

The weed rocks

Seascape

one is unsuitable, you can choose another with similar capabilities that will be all right.

A further textural aspect is how the objects that surround us are useful in the creation of design ideas. As you look at the wonderful craggy surface of the weathered bark of a venerable tree, you can develop a textural composition along similar lines. The possibilities are endless once you begin to really get involved with the literally thousands of textures, patterns, and their inspirations for design.

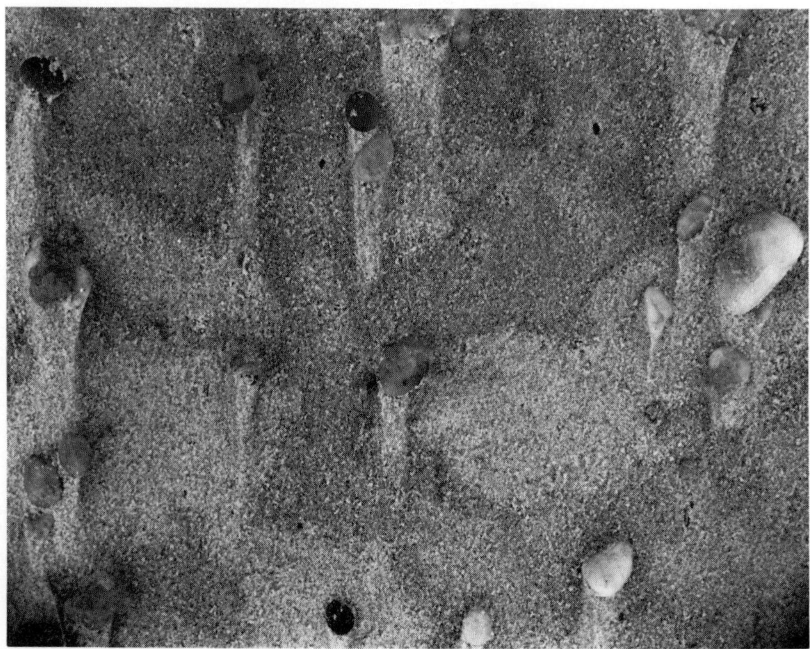

Tracings

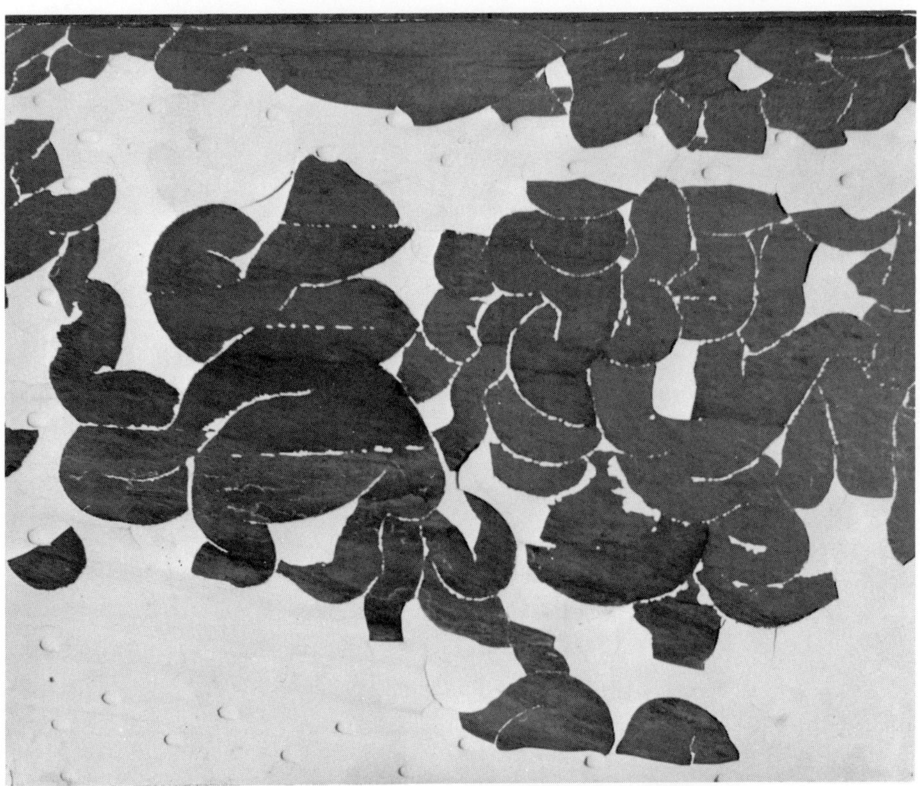

Textural design compositions. *Photos by Martin Last*

CHAPTER FIVE

Planning The Final Design

NOW THAT YOU HAVE BECOME more familiar with the concepts of design, the question naturally arises how to develop them in your own work. You have seen how to create a balanced design, how colors go together, and the textural aspects of design. Now you will want to begin applying these techniques.

The basis of a well-planned design is experience and experimentation. And of course, as you work you will keep the qualities of the medium you enjoy in mind, remembering that they should remain expressive of themselves in the completed object.

In needlework, weaving, batik and other textile-related crafts, the ultimate product is often flat, and therefore somewhat like a textural painting. In this case, it will be easy to plan the design on paper, which is also two dimensional. When designing for a more three dimensional medium, like ceramics or the soft scultpures made from pliant materials, you will want to do two or more views of the article on paper so that your finished design encompasses all sides.

If your design idea is pretty well defined in your mind, you can begin to interpret it on paper. If you are not sure, consult various sources of idea and inspiration. Look at works of art with themes you like. Study them in books, museums and libraries. Keep your mind open to new concepts. Be flexible while seeing how others have expressed themselves.

Every day you come into contact with literally hundreds of articles that have designs and patterns. The flowers in a print fabric, the paisley on a shawl, the edging on a plate, all can provide jumping off points for new designs of your own. It is interesting to pause and see how the elements and principles of design have been applied to the things you see.

In a varied print with several motifs there may be only one that is of particular interest to you. Study it and see why it caught your eye. Was it the color? The shape? The texture? Is it a nice unit in itself? Asking these questions will help you understand just what it was that appealed to you and will be useful in the formulation of your own ideas.

Make a visual record of the motifs and design elements that you like. Sketch anything that is of note. Or make a quick written reminder of what it was you liked about something you saw. Save snips of patterned cloth, photographs, pictures in magazines, old prints, engravings or pages from antiquated books. When you begin a new design, go through your collection to spark ideas in yourself.

Printed Victorian children's blocks, each side of the block going to make up part of a different design, among the hundreds of idea inspirations that surround us

You can select the design elements that you prefer and blend them together in original ways. If you feel that your sketching ability is not up to par, get some good tracing paper, known as layout paper or vellum. Use it to compile and redraw motifs. That way you do not have to redo the whole design each time you want to change it. You can continue to recopy just the parts that need a finishing touch until they look right. You can also cut out and put together individual sketches to form a whole. Once they are assembled on the page in a pleasing layout, you can trace the entire grouping without disturbing the arrangement.

Whenever you receive a publication of any sort—a magazine, seed or flower catalogue—look through it for design elements. Clip and save them, or trace the ones that cannot be cut up. As you go on, your collection will grow and you will be surprised at how many ideas you will want to try.

If you see something that is rare or delicate, make a photostat or photocopy. Museums often sell postcards and other reproductions of works in their collections. You can buy ones that are particularly interesting so that you can consult and refer to them later on, without having to rely entirely on memory.

The basic aim of collecting and saving all sorts of materials like these is to build your frame of reference as you compile a visual record. Anything that offers food for thought is useful as you create a backlog of information that you can call upon at any time.

To plan the design itself, assemble the materials you need—pencils, drawing paper, tracing paper, erasers, marking pens, water color paints, tape, ruler, etc. Begin to work by making a series of small outlines on a sheet of paper that are the same shape as the project. Work out various design possibilities in these thumbnail sketches. You will be able to visualize the design without having to draw a large version every time. These small plans also allow you to try out as many schemes as you like, using a minimum of time and space.

When you have reached the basic idea, make a plan of the actual dimensions of your project. As an intermediate step, you can make a half-size version to check last minute details. If your work will cover a large area, you can reduce the size, while keeping the proportions constant, to draw the design. When the design is complete, you can enlarge it easily, using one of several methods. If you are making an article that must be assembled when finished, do not forget to allow for seams, borders or any other excess material needed within the design outlines, so that they are not left out until it is too late to put them back in.

When you have a good proportional sketch or other plan, it is easy to enlarge it to the exact size of the object. You will not only be able to see how it looks in the finished size, but you will have an excellent guide or pattern to follow while you complete the project.

The easiest way to make an enlargement is to take your design to a photographic store and ask for an enlarged photostatic copy. Tell them the exact size you want and ask for both the positive—black lines on white paper, and negative—white lines on black paper. If you do not specify this you will probably just get the negative version which may be hard to work from and cannot be colored in later. Also, having both on hand will be useful as they will show you how negative space is used in your design. Generally, a well-planned design will look equally good in both versions.

Unfortunately, enlarging with photostats only works when your design is already in the correct proportions. If, for example, the small version is 6″ x 9″ and you want it to be 12″ x 18″, you can do a photostat and it will come out right. To change the proportions, you can enlarge the design yourself. Make a copy of the design that you don't mind drawing on. Use a ruler and divide the edges of the design into equal parts. An inch wide is usually a good size to use. Then draw vertical and horizontal lines following your measured sections, so that the design is covered with a series of inch square boxes that form a grid.

If the edges are not easily divided into an even set of inches so that there is a fraction left over, you can use a ruler to divide them into equal sections. Hold it firmly on a corner of the design, with the ruler running along the edge you want to divide. Move the other end of the ruler up a bit on a slant until an even inch measurement shows up at that end. You may only need to move the ruler a fraction of an inch

Positive and negative photostats of the design unit for a fabric by Nancy Greenberg and the author.

to accomplish this. Then, work across the ruler, marking a dot on the design at each inch on the ruler. Use these dots to draw your lines and they will be equally spaced, even if they are not exactly an inch apart. Do the same for the other side edge if necessary.

Then take a sheet of paper at least as large as the enlarged design will be. Mark the outlines of the desired design enlargement on it. Then, divide the sides into the same number of lines as the smaller version and draw a grid on it as you did on the smaller one. If, for example, your new design will be twice as large, make the boxes in the grid two inches square. The important thing is to obtain the same number of boxes, regardless of their actual size. If you are enlarging something a lot, say four or five times, it may be helpful to do it in two stages instead of trying to make such a big step all at once.

Place the outlined large sheet of paper and the small design on a table which is a convenient height to draw on. Start at any box in the larger grid and carefully copy the outlines of the design that appear in the corresponding box on the small design. After you do the major outlines, fill in the details. Work box by box until the entire design has been copied and enlarged. Even if you do not draw, breaking up the design into small sections like this somehow makes it easier.

To change proportions, this method works automatically as you include the same number of boxes in each size of the design. As you draw within them, the shapes and forms of the design naturally stretch themselves out, accommodating themselves to the new proportion without too much trouble. In the larger version, the grid you marked as squares on the smaller one may come out as rectangles, but this is correct as long as there are the same number of boxes.

Enlarging with a grid

Enlarged version with a grid

To enlarge round, oval or irregularly shaped designs this way, enclose the shape in an outlined square or rectangle, whichever it will fit into best. Then proceed as above, using a larger square or rectangle for the large version. When you are finished, the design will be enlarged and you can ignore or erase the extra outline.

Changing proportions with a grid enlargement

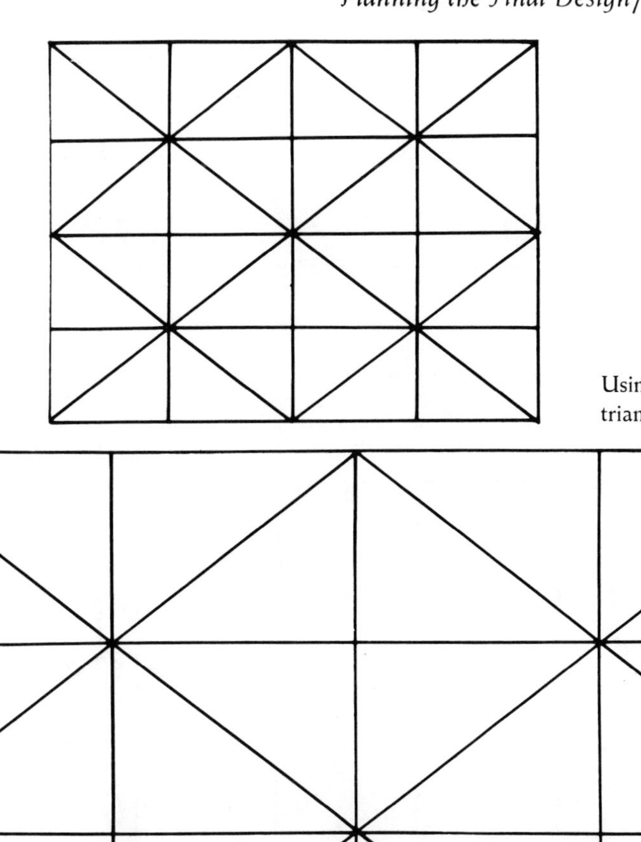

Using a triangle grid

Another method of enlargement that is quite similar and works equally well is to form a grid of triangular shapes by drawing two sets of diagonal lines that cross each other and one set of horizontal lines to make the triangles. You then mark off the larger outlines, draw an equal number of triangles for the grid in much the same way the boxes were formed in the previous method. Then copy the sections one at a time, starting with the bold outlines and adding details when they are done.

Whichever method you use, if you want a clear copy of the enlarged design to work from, cover the design with a sheet of tracing paper and redraw it.

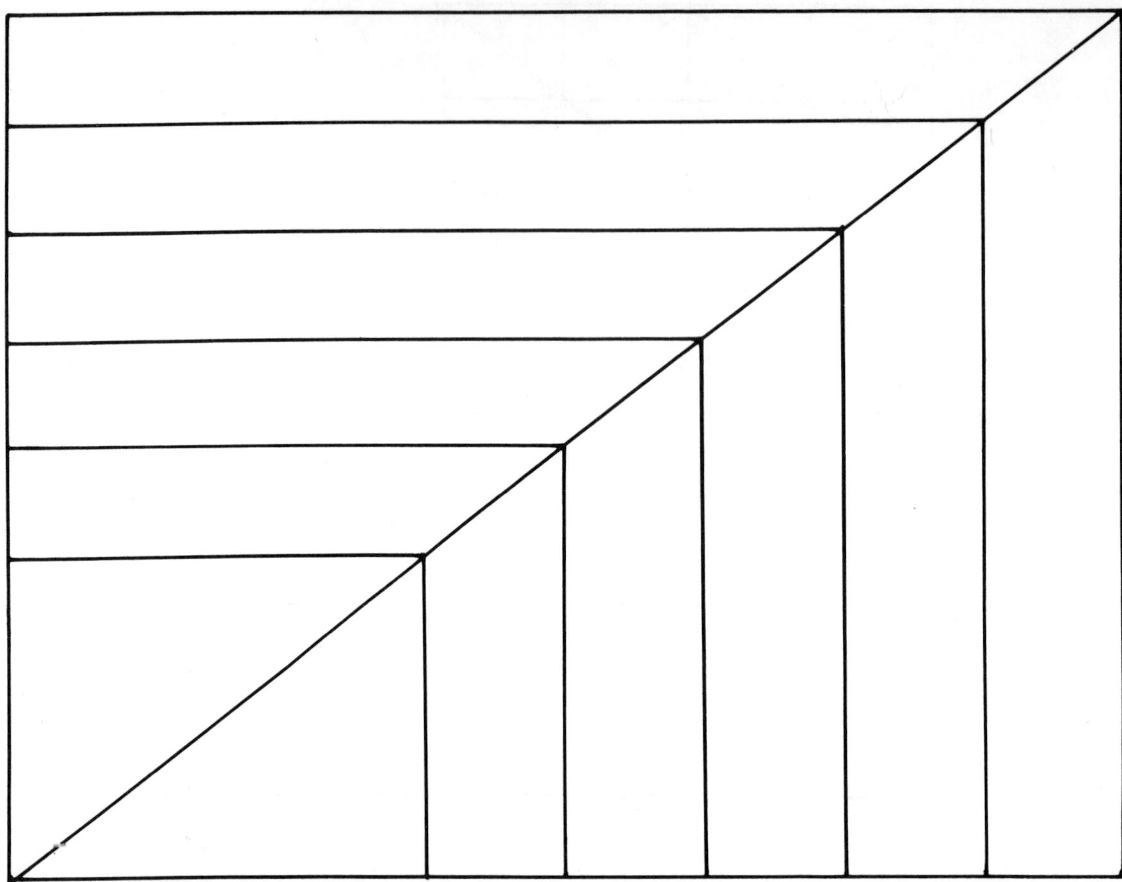

Extending the sides of a rectangle with a diagonal line

Sometimes you will want to enlarge a rectangular or square outline without changing the proportions or having to figure out the final lengths of sides, top and bottom mathematically. To do this, get a sheet of paper large enough for the final version. Place the design on the lower left hand corner of the paper, lining up the corner and the two edges of design and paper that meet there. Draw a diagonal line with a ruler, leading from the lower left corner of the design to the upper right hand corner. Extend it on the paper underneath, carefully following it out on the same angle. Then, measure off the dimensions you want on one edge of the larger sheet of paper. Draw a line up to meet the diagonal line on the paper. Then you can draw a line from the point where the two meet to the other edge and you will have a new rectangle that is in the same proportions as the original. By forming two new sides using the diagonal line as the new upper right hand corner, you can make any size rectangle in the same proportions as your original model.

For color guidelines, you can add them to the enlarged final version of your design with water paint, crayon, colored pencils or felt tip markers. If you buy the markers in an art supply store, you will find them in an amazing range of colors that are easy to apply and attractive. To experiment, have several photocopies made of your final design and color them in, using various color schemes. Then you can select the one that you like best. If you want to just indicate the colors, dab a bit of color within each outline of a design form or shape. But for a really good view of the finished pattern, fill it in entirely, the way it will look when completed.

You can use the final design as a guide to work on the project. If you are working in a medium where the ultimate product can be worked over a rendering of the design, as in needlepoint canvas, you can draw or trace the design directly onto the net. Be sure that the ink or felt tip pen you use is absolutely waterproof. No matter what it says on its label, mark a scrap and test it before using. To mark a design for this kind of work, place the canvas over the design and draw right on it. If it is hard to see, hold it up to a bright window or use a glass table with a light underneath. Draw the outlines first and when you are sure they are right, add details. If you do not want to ruin the original design while tracing, put a section of a dry cleaner's plastic bag or sheet of clear household wrap in between the design and the canvas. Then you will be able to see it just as well and the marker or ink won't drip through onto the design itself. Indicate the colors with bits of yarn or paint them in with thinned acrylic paint. To thin the paint, use its own medium, not water, which will mess up the canvas.

Other methods of indicating a design on fabric include using carbon paper, transfer pencils or dressmakers' chalk. The chalk comes in many colors for contrast and rubs off when you are finished or if you need to correct a line.

To work with a paper design in other crafts, make it as easy to follow as possible, using bold outlines and clearly delineated colors. Whenever possible, indicate the method used—a different stitch or weave, for example, right on the paper pattern. Many weavers, who work in the more figurative tapestry technique, place a full sized model of the design behind the upright warp threads of their loom.

The plan for indicating a design may not be as simple in many types of work, but you can make templates for tracing around in some cases; in other cases you will depend on your eyes and just look back and forth from design to project. You can choose the best method to suit yourself.

CHAPTER SIX

Sources Of Design Inspiration In The Fine Arts

THE FINE ARTS ARE AN aesthetic chronicle of our civilization that provide us with an endless source of pattern and design inspiration. You will discover birds, beasts, and flowers, borders, symbols and signs. All of the flora and fauna of life's surroundings as seen and interpreted throughout history by the eyes and hands of our ancestors are found in art. An awe-inspiring heritage handed down to us from the beginning of recorded experience, it is a bottomless well of visual stimuli that can help spark your imagination by opening your eyes to new and original applications for your own work.

The concepts and images are as varied and exciting as the peoples they spring from, so that no one book can possibly hope to present all of the potentials within each culture. What is intended here is an introduction to the basic arts of the ages along with selected photographic and pictorial examples to assist you in the choice of design areas that interest you. In the back of the book is a list of pictorial reference books, providing additional research materials so that you can pursue the design aspects of the arts you enjoy.

As we look at the works of times past, there are some fundamental questions that can be answered, to give us a fuller insight into the actual processes of art and design: the techniques and materials employed, the point of view of the artists as well as the function of the articles themselves, the environment that produced the desire for these things and the stylistic influences of other civilizations. These will provide you with a more flexible base of understanding regarding the application of various design motifs and patterns.

You do not need to have any background in the arts to study and profit from them enjoyably. What is important is to pay attention to the fine details in a painting or other work of art, along with the impact of the work as a whole. Particularly in the representational works of the earlier days, the artists were very careful to choose decorative units that would further enhance the theme of their work. In this way, when a manuscript illuminator of the Middle Ages or a painter of the early Renaissance depicted a scene, he painstakingly planned the smallest detail in dress, objects and surroundings. The print on a fabric, the architectural carving on a building, the flower quietly growing in a corner, all are part of the entirety; at the same time they stand on their own to perhaps suggest a single design motif or segment that interests you.

These motifs are often depictions of the decorative arts of the day. They can inspire other forms, layouts and patterns that you may want to adapt into your own designs. By studying the lesser parts, within the work as a whole, you will enhance your appreciation of the fine arts themselves while adding to the store of knowledge that is the foundation of your individual interpretations. As you look, you may become aware of the recurring characteristics of certain styles and periods. For example, you might find that a certain type of motif constantly catches your eye. Keep a sketched or photographic record of the things you like and you will probably discover that one, or more, periods in particular show up. From there, it is relatively simple to explore other examples within the area you feel a preference for. You can then seek out other works that contributed to that style. Before you know it, you will have an entire background on a period in art or a civilization that you find stimulating, while refining your own style.

This method of studying inspirational works of art becomes easier all the time. Many fine art books are published with accurate reproductions in black and white and color, as well as enlargements of detailed sections of the works shown. Because these books can be quite expensive to collect, your library card will become an invaluable passport into the world of art.

If there is an art museum nearby, make good use of it. Go, look around, see what type of works they have on display. Almost all of the major cities in the United States contain at least one fine arts museum and they are very informative and stimulating to both our purposes and life in general. There are also many museums that specialize in one area, medium, group or period. If you are unable to go in person, museums often publish catalogues of their major exhibits and acquisitions and permanent collections. They are usually not as expensive as formal art books and most contain information and illustrations of the works and sometimes offer additional material on the artists or periods depicted. You can keep track of the current exhibits and shows in your area through the listings in the newspapers, or in magazines, if you are in a larger city. And don't forget the art galleries. Although their works are for sale, you do not have to buy anything and most galleries welcome browsers. Many local schools, colleges and clubs hold exhibitions of their members' work which can keep you in touch with what is being done by today's artists and artisans.

Historic houses, landmarks and recreations of past villages also provide good searching grounds for design and pattern. They present a realistic setting as you see all of the objects and decorative arts of everyday life accompanying the works of fine art. The hand-carved wooden scroll work above doors and windows, a pattern in a curtain or the rooster on a weathervane are all inspirational as they give a glowing impression of another era.

To aid us further in our search through the past for design suggestions, there are generally divisible periods in art and design. They are usually classified as: Prehistoric, which includes the Stone Ages and seems to end with the development of writing in various places; Ancient, which includes the Golden Age of Greece and the Roman Empire as well as the earlier Egyptian, Near Eastern, and Minoan civilizations; Byzantine, which includes the Near Eastern Roman Empire and its vast influence on the European period often known as the Dark Ages, from the fall of Rome in 476 A.D. until about the year 900; the Medieval Period, including the later Dark Ages and the period up until the fifteenth century known as the Middle Ages; the Renaissance, or rebirth of knowledge and culture in the West; Asian Art, including China, Japan, India and related countries; and Modern Art, which takes us up to the present. Naturally, there are numerous subdivisions and cultures that are not tied in as directly, but these categories provide an easy breakdown with which we can follow the continuum of art and design.

You will find that nothing ever happens in only one place. Remarkable similarities of motif and style seem to occur in unrelated areas of the world. Simultaneous developments appear in different places at the same time, and conversely, if an age of accomplishment ends in one area, it might not yet have begun in another.

PREHISTORIC ART

The animals portrayed in the famous cave paintings of southern France and northern Spain seem ample proof of humanity's constant

Sketch of a painting from the caves at Lascaux, France

desire for more esthetic surroundings. Their shape and mass are deceptively simple yet strong in impact. A cave dweller's vision of a pre-historic animal can be a striking theme, whether it is painted, baked and glazed, carved or stitched.

This early art, or design, was concerned with the facts of day-to-day existence for the Cro Magnon peoples of the Old Stone Age. If the supply of animals dwindled, the tribes were forced to move on, or die out. But the desire to depict this necessity of their lives was something more than pure survival. Perhaps their designs were intended to insure the success of the hunt, or they were done by those unable to participate. We will never know the real reasons, although we do know that they were involved in the creation of realistic, colorful images that call out for crafts interpretation.

ART IN THE ANCIENT WORLD

The first great civilizations of Egypt and Mesopotamia began to record history in the Nile and Tigris-Euphrates river valleys. In Egypt, the writing took the form of hieroglyphics, based on pictures of the word forms. Each figure in itself is a design that might be adapted as part of a whole or as an individual study. The Mesopotamian writings were wedge-shaped cuneiform letters done on clay tablets. They were made around 5,000 to 4,000 B.C.

By 3,000 B.C., the Egyptian civilization was pretty much in the

Birds from an Egyptian painting

form we have come to know. Their vast system of buildings were covered with scenes and decorations that are alive with exotic figurations.

The arts of pottery, weaving, jewelry making, carving and wall painting were quite advanced and countless picture books on them are available for study. The mechanics of perspective were unknown at the time and they could not depict it realistically. However, that somehow seems to add to the unique quality of their designs. When something was meant to be farther away, they placed it at the top of the scene. Almost all figures shown are in profile from the neck up and legs down, with the central portion of the body facing forward. The forms used are flat, without shading, and are colored in the same hues over and over. There is abundant use of symbolism and a very linear style that seems to lend itself to practical application. Egyptian

Egyptian Reproductions, Dyn. XVIII, C. 1415 B.C. Wall Painting: Fishing and Fowling; from the tomb of Menena, Scribe of the Fields of the Lord of the Two Lands. *The Metropolitan Museum of Art*

art was rediscovered during the French Empire period and the stylized flowers and animal forms adapted then are still of interest to designers today.

In sculpture, the lack of perspective is somewhat less apparent but the statues of people are very static, with the greatest motion represented by the placement of the left foot forward. The carved bodies are so still that you can almost see the original block of stone in its square or columnar shape prior to carving.

In the Mesopotamian region, the Babylonian Sumerian peoples followed a different course. Their art was concerned with conquest and it commemorated the warriors with their more heavy-set bodies than those seen in Egyptian renderings. They did not have a greater knowledge of perspective, but otherwise the contributions of the various Near Eastern groups of this area were many. They were known for

Drawing of a Near Eastern Jug, from about 2,000 B.C.

their fine work in carved and set jewels and fine weaving. They added the concept of a vaulted ceiling supported by arches to architecture. The Syrian Hittites are thought to be the first to use iron, heralding a new age. The Phoenicians developed the alphabet, which in itself is a form of applied design, and spread the cultures of Babylon and Egypt throughout the known world through their extensive Mediterranean sea trade routes, which even reached and influenced the lands on the northeastern Atlantic Ocean.

The designs of the Aegean peoples, especially those in Crete, manifested many elements of Babylonian art in their later civilization. The palace of Minos at Knossos was worked on for centuries and finally completed about 1,500 B.C. Its walls were covered with paintings that are lively and colorful to this day. Beginning to feel the necessity of showing perspective, the Minoans tried to foreshorten the bodies of people depicted on their excellent decorative pottery.

The Minoan style is still linear, using flat outlined subjects filled in with bright colors, in spite of the attempts at perspective in some cases. The flowing curved lines and organic elements are a bit freer and more responsive to natural forms than those of many previous cultures. You will find their colorful style and content suitable to countless interpretations.

Typical Greek figure

In Ancient Greece, the Periclean Age is often thought of as the epitome of learning and culture. Within the span of the several centuries that comprised it there were a tremendous number of scientific and artistic achievements. In all areas, the love of learning was expressed. The products of this Classic Age in painting, sculpture and architecture have been felt as an influence over the centuries, with many revivals and Neo-Classic periods occurring as they were rediscovered by later generations and peoples.

As the strength and power of Greece grew, there was a concomitant growth in all of the art forms. Here we find examples of the development of mechanical perspective for the first time in recorded history, accompanied by the realism in form and the use of light and shadow that is so effective. The vase paintings are the only ones that survive although we know from the writings of the time that the walls were richly painted and decorated. The ceramics in themselves are of note as they show a use of pattern and design that truly enhance their form. Their borders are carefully worked and the Greek key border, so prevalent in crafts design, is but one of the inspirational patterns that can be found in the art of this age. As you look at a Grecian urn, remember that in Grecian times it was not something that was kept on display. Rather, it was a functional example of a useful ceramic that was decorated for the added enjoyment of its users.

Mosaics were also worked and still exist, giving us an idea of how realistic and detailed the wall paintings must have been. The scenes

Greek style border motif

V Century B.C. Athenian Red-figured Pottery. Early free style. Volute Krater: about 450 B.C. On Body: A and B. Battle of Greeks and Amazons. On neck: A. Combat of Lapiths and centaurs at Wedding Feast of Peirithous. B. Youth calling girl. Attributed to the Painter of the Woolly Satyrs. *The Metropolitan Museum of Art, Rogers Fund*, 1907.

are like ceramic tapestries, laden with color and content. In sculpture, the body began to move and turn as the artist learned how to carve realistically. This love of realism produced an element that is surprising. The pure whiteness that we associate with the statues of this era is mainly due to the ravages of time as most of them were painstakingly painted and the years have worn off the original coloration. By 350 B.C., the art of sculpture seems to reach a physical perfection as the Greeks delighted in carving the ideal in beauty.

The characteristic columnar style of architecture developed and the columns and capitals were given the names of the people who contributed to them, and to Greek culture as a whole. Although these orders of architecture are thought of as chronological, the use of one did not preclude the continued use of the previous style. The three styles are easily recognizable; the Doric has a simple rounded form, the Ionic has a curved scroll like a top and the Corinthian is the most complex, with an intricate acanthus leaf embellishment. The columns were augmented by richly carved friezes, often painted in vibrant colors. Within the carved columns and facades we can find many small figures and depictions of plant forms that lend the feeling of Classic style to many modern works.

The Hellenistic period ended with the expansion of the power of Rome and the creation of the Roman Empire. The Greek culture was, however, absorbed by its conquerors and had a great influence on the style of Rome. They followed the Greek ideals in the beauty of art and architecture completely at first, until their own style began to evolve through trial, error and interpretation, just as yours can.

Another earlier culture that added to the Roman design concepts was that of Etruria. By 800 B.C., the Etruscans had settled in the part of Italy that is now Tuscany. They had many Near Eastern and Greek

Figure from an Etruscan tomb at Tarquinia.

Roman Mosaics. Second half of II Century A.D. From Antioch. From Roman villa at Daphne. Mosaic pavement: central panel. Personification of Spring. *Metropolitan Museum of Art, Purchase, 1938, Joseph Pulitzer Bequest*

characteristics. As they flourished, they made many bright, colorful ceramics, bronze works and tomb paintings.

The Romans conquered the Etruscans along with the entire Mediterranean region and by later periods extended their empire to include what is now England as well as much of Europe, northern Africa and the Middle East. The Romans were collectors through conquest and brought many prizes of vanquished cultures home. Much of our knowledge of Greek sculpture comes from this booty. They also imported Greek painters until their own developed later on. Mosaics, murals and wall paintings were realistic, incorporating perspective and real space. Their mosaic style in particular seems to lend itself readily to interpretation in many craft forms.

The extensive knowledge we have of Roman civilization was provided by the volcanic eruption that destroyed Pompeii and Herculaneum in 79 A.D. These outlying suburbs of Rome were preserved almost intact by layers of volcanic ash and other material. When carefully excavated centuries later, they revealed a rich source of art and design. In Rome itself, the only paintings of this period that still exist are found in underground catacombs, those that were made on walls of houses and temples having been destroyed by time.

One of the great Roman contributions in achitecture and engineering was the combined use of the modes of the Greek and Etruscan, producing an arch, vault and dome out of the primitive arch of the Etruscans and the columns of the Greeks. As military conquerors, they built roads, bridges and aqueducts wherever they went to speed men and supplies along a vast network of the first highways.

As scholars and artists, the Romans developed the first illuminated books, in the form of a codex, or long folded strip of paper that was bound at one edge, somewhat like a modern book. This tradition was to be developed later by the monks of the Medieval Era.

The fabulous tradition of decorative design, opulence and wealth that was Rome at its height gradually declined but their rich legacy of creative assimilation is happily available to us for study. The final blow to the staggering Empire came in 476 A.D., when Germanic barbarian hordes sacked the city.

BYZANTINE ART AND THE EARLY MEDIEVAL PERIOD

In the early 4th century, the Roman Empire was in two sections, with an Eastern half at Byzantium, which is now Istanbul, in the Near East. The Empire embraced Christianity in 313 by an edict of the Emperor Constantine. As the capital in the East, Byzantium was renamed Constantinople in his honor, although the art style is known as Byzantine.

When the Western Empire fell in the next century, the Eastern half remained strong and became the center of learning and the repository for the culture that had been Rome. After its fall, the pursuit and furtherance of art and learning were all but forgotten in Western Europe. The great advances of the Greek and Roman days lay dormant and unused. The illumination of manuscripts became widespread there as they preserved the knowledge and literature of the West.

The use of gold and lavish embellishment of the manuscripts was derived from the enormous mosaics that covered the walls of their early Christian churches. The mosaic tesserae were made of marble or glass and gold leaf. The coloration was bright and opulent, adding a richness to the basically flat appearance of the two dimensional shapes of the depicted scenes. This application of brilliant color is a

Romanesque vault and arch

valuable lesson to us in the use of hue to produce dramatic effects that could be used in any area of craft endeavor.

During the early Medieval Age in the West, almost all building that took place was done for the Christian Church. The style became known as Romanesque, or after the Roman, and a few castles and forts were built following its lines. It was actually a fusion of the Roman and Germanic influences. The Romanesque buildings were made of massive blocks of stone, often carved with many low relief sculptures. These sculptures are an interesting study in texture and shape. The vault and arch were prevalent. The monasetries became the centers of art and learning. Within their cloistered walls, patient monks labored to copy and preserve the knowledge of earlier times in writing rooms known as scriptoria. Book illuminations were the major art of the day and they became more elaborate as the monks' skill increased. In particular, the first letter on each page grew in size and embellishment. Also included were miniatures or small paintings that enhanced the text. Along the edges of a page or to fill in lines of uneven length, monks drew leaves and plants, fine scroll work, and sometimes human or other figures. In keeping with the beauty of hand-lettered parchment pages, the bindings were finely wrought in enamels, precious metals and jewels. Stained glass also came into use to enliven solid stone with the gleam of color and pattern.

THE MIDDLE AGES

The latter half of the Medieval period, generally called the Middle Ages, includes the years from about 900–1,500. Guilds of artisans developed to set style and quality and teach their techniques to following generations through a system of apprenticeship. During this time, art was an expression of faith that is often characterized as Gothic piety. Concerned as it was with the church it produced great ecclesiastical works in the form of illuminations, stained glass, enamel work, metal work and tapestries. They were executed in flat shapes, with masses of unshaded color filled into black outlines.

Many of these works were also made for the castles of feudal lords, as were the ornate suits of armor, heraldic banners and other identifying marks for the endless series of battles. The shields and motifs of heraldry continue to be a popular theme for personalized designs. The flags, family coats of arms and even the tracery on armor are a rich vein of ornamental design, just waiting to be tapped and expanded upon.

One of the creative marvels of history is the depiction in needle and thread of the invasion and conquest of England by the Norman William the Conqueror in 1066 at the Battle of Hastings, as presented in the famous Bayeux Tapestry. It probably was made within a few years of the event and is actually an epic embroidery done in separate strips which were sewn together afterwards. The stitched shapes of the opposing armies are beautifully worked and tell the entire story in fascinating detail. Each section contains a variety of design elements and is a tale in itself.

Knights, horses, the fruits of the land are presented simply but effectively. This work is further proof that your own work need not be

Nancy P. Dryfoos. Stitchery

Mary Ann Scherr. "Ulmeck" Pre-Columbian stone, ostrich feathers, ivory, fur, gold, silver

Margaret Sussman. Box 2″ diameter, silver and cloisonné enamel

Nancy Belfer. "Vine Forms," 17″x17″

Bernadyne Antin. "Gears and Chromosomes" Punch needle on homespun backing. 33″x38″

Kurt E. Fishback. "Vegetable Plate," 1972, enamel on ceramic, 15″

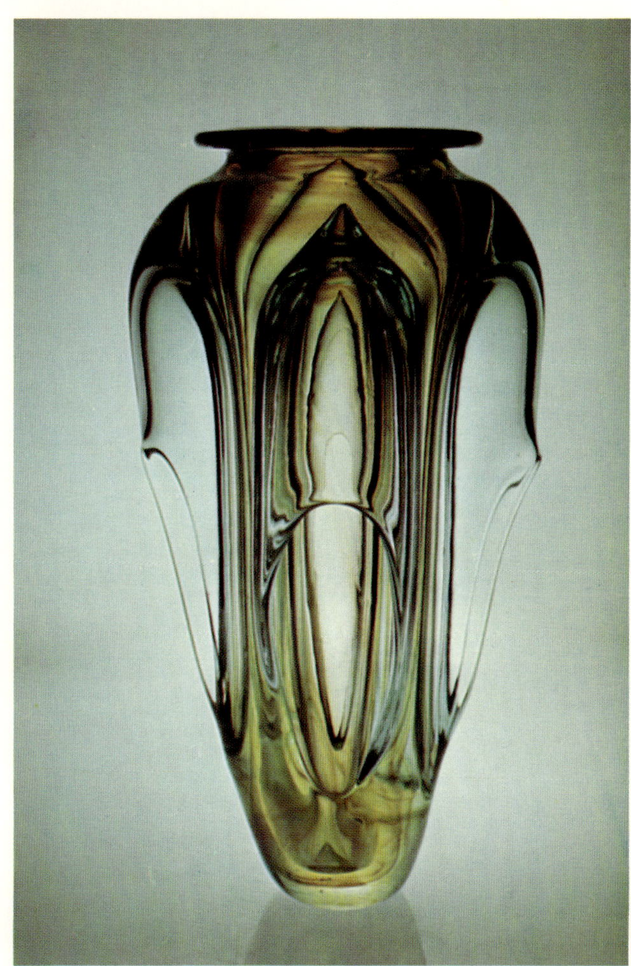
Tom Mcglauchlin. Vase with four bubbles. Silver yellow cased with clear. 1973

Renie B. Adams. "Still Life with a Picture on the Wall," 1973, (shown in scale next to a life sized crocheted egg). Stitchery on a crocheted form. Silk on linen, 5″x3″x2¾″

Kay Whitcomb. "Flight"
Plique-a-jour set in Flicker box.
14″x15″

John Lewis. Moon Bottles

Etel Adnen. Woven by Hal Painier, Collection, Artist

Joseph Almyda. Batik, Linen with organdy overlays, 3′x4′

Heraldic shields

photographic in order to convey the ideas and concepts you've envisioned.

The crusades of the eleventh to thirteenth centuries were a jolt to the somnolence of Western Europe. Their influences on the Eastern life and culture were many and varied. Artists and scholars were brought back to the West with the remnants of returning armies and the exchange of ideas was renewed. Money began to circulate again and towns and cities grew through trade in silks and spices. The love of learning was reinstated in many areas and universities came into being.

The Romanesque style merged with that of the Byzantine so that the bright colors and flat forms were included in mosaics of churches in Europe, particularly in Italy. These are both decorative and colorful, showing a use of two-dimensional shapes that can be well suited to designs for works in the fiber arts.

The possibilities of building were enhanced as the use of pointed arches, vaults and spires eventually led to a new style, later known as Gothic. It was a term of disparagement at first, being named after the Goths, a barbarous, conquering northern tribe. The title is not very accurate, but it is entrenched in the lexicon of design.

The twelfth and thirteenth centuries are marked by the construction of great cathedrals with an overwhelming feeling of height and inspiration, due to the upward thrust of Gothic architecture. Stone walls were replaced by pillars. Cathedrals included stained glass windows in sparkling hues which can be used to date the period as they progressively became more complex and ornate. Windows such as the Rose Window in Notre Dame de Paris are unsurpassed in their kaleidoscopic pattern and coloration and can provide us with an example of the development of a radiating design.

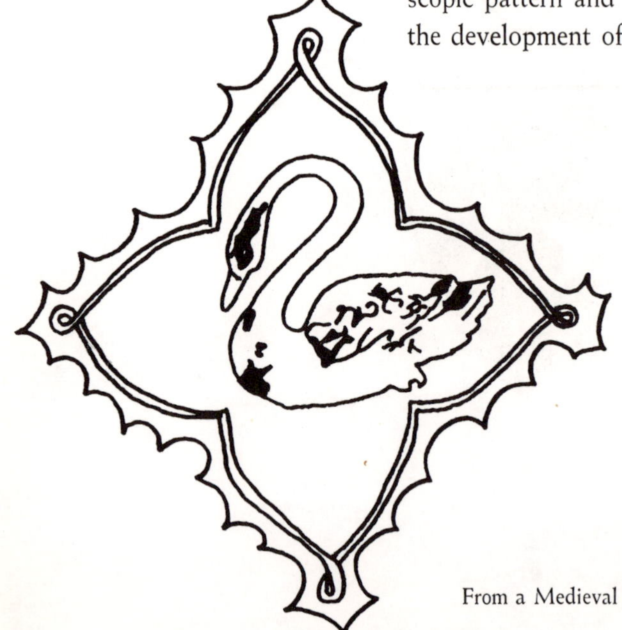

From a Medieval manuscript

Gothic pointed vaults and arches

Sketch from a mosaic at Ravenna, Italy

From an inlaid marble table of the Italian Renaissance

THE RENAISSANCE

For those who are taken with the vibrant use of color, coupled with grace and beauty of execution—and who isn't—the Renaissance provides a rich source of design motivation. The works of Botticelli alone contain enough substance to keep even the most prolific imaginations busy. And he is just one of the masters of that glorious era in art whose works are available for present day contemplation.

As people became more aware of their world, Medieval Europe began to feel the winds of change. With the ultimate collapse of Constantinople in the fifteenth century, the fleeing emigrants helped reinstate the Classic ideals and knowledge brought with them as they resettled in the West. Their added impetus had much to do with the rebirth of learning in the Renaissance.

At first, the Renaissance was centered in the Italian city of Florence, where merchants had grown rich through trade. They became patrons of the arts, desirous of enhancing their sumptuous homes with portraits and landscapes as well as depictions of Biblical themes. The growing awareness of light and shadow, called chiaroscuro, and perspective foreshadowed the works of great artists like Michaelangelo, Leonardo da Vinci, Botticelli and Raphael.

By the time of the High Renaissance, in the late fifteenth and sixteenth centuries, the events that started in Florence and spread to the rest of Italy began to change the face of Europe. The Northern countries had their own Renaissance, as expressed in the works of masters of painting like Rembrandt van Rijn.

Building was done at an unparalleled pace. The new emphasis was on man and his works. Sculptors of the day studied classical examples as painters concentrated on realism, a classical ideal. The human figure in painting became real as the techniques of light and shadow and the illusion of space were employed to their fullest. The flat shapes of the Medieval period were now three-dimensional forms, with mass and weight. Paintings came into their own as new subjects were introduced.

Fine works in tapestry and embroidery techniques were made in many countries. They also included an attention to realistic detail, such as the flowers depicted in the renowned Unicorn Tapestries. These are so vividly and correctly executed that their exact species can be identified. Each one can be a study in the use of floral forms in crafts.

The Renaissance made many contributions in all spheres of learning and technology, which were to have continuing impact. The introduction of printing, the use of popular languages in writing instead of Latin, Galileo's invention of the telescope and the resulting Copernican theory of the universe were among these outstanding achievements.

As the Renaissance subsided, the Reformation began to change European ideas still further. A new style, following the emotional qualities of motion in paintings by artists like Rubens, was called Baroque. The expressive Baroque style is marked by movement and a turn from formal balance to asymmetric composition; it can be seen in the works of Caravaggio in Italy and Velasquez in Spain.

DESIGN DEVELOPMENTS IN THE SEVENTEENTH AND EIGHTEENTH CENTURIES

In the seventeenth century, the American colonial people began to undergo increasing independence from English style. The earliest settlers often adapted the methods of the native Indians that were so well suited to the land. The colonials learned to make do for themselves, creating their own clothing, furniture, tools and eventually, designs as well. The early Jacobean design influence was strong, but it lessened as the uniquely American motifs and patterns were developed and used. These colonial themes are still popular today, as are the Jacobean stylized flowers, and provide fine traditional designs.

Among the many colonial products were carved ship's figureheads, signs, pewter and brass work. Paintings done by unsophisticated folk artists known as limners were two dimensional and quite decorative in

D. J. Holmes, "The Great Seal of the State of Maine", 27″ x 31″. Carved for the remodeled governor's office in the statehouse, Augusta, Maine. Dedicated, November, 1972. Basswood, polychromed and gold leaf; Black Cherry, stain. *Courtesy, Artist*

Left, French or Flemish, Late XV Century, *The Hunt of the Unicorn*, VII: *The Unicorn in Captivity*. Wool and silk with metal threads. From the Chateau of Verteuil. *The Metropolitan Museum of Art, The Cloisters Collection, Gift of John D. Rockefeller, Jr.*, 1937.

American, Mid-19th Century. Coverlet: Album Quilt, cotton and some wool 6′11″ x 7′1″. *The Metropolitan Museum of Art, Posthumous gift of Miss Eliza Polhemus Cobb (through Mrs. Arthur Bunker)*, 1952

their use of color and composition. Often the background and figure for a portrait were painted prior to meeting the subject and these artists were also called face painters for this reason.

Colonial wives and daughters made many of the home furnishings, and their thrifty improvisations led to the widespread use of techniques for reworking used materials into colorful patchwork quilts and hooked rugs. They also made much of their own cloth and did embroideries, adding comfort and beauty to their homes. By the time of the War for Independence, America had a style all its own. The recently developed patriotic motifs such as eagles and flags reflected a growing identification with the individuality of the new land.

Cornucopia and turkey, typical American motifs

Meanwhile, in Europe, the rulers of wealthy nations increased their own power to the extent that they became absolute. Under Louis XIVth, seventeenth century France set the classic style standard throughout Europe. While he weakened the purses of the French nobility by forcing them to live at court and emulate his sumptuous life style, France became the center of art and fashion. This was to continue for many years afterwards.

By the eighteenth century, the depiction of life at court was expressed in the style known as Rococo. It was a reaction against the pompous, later-Baroque style and used rock and shell-like forms in architecture and decoration. Rococo paintings were light and gay with playful cupids, shepherds and lovely maidens, frolicking in billowing landscapes. These were themes that recall a longing for simpler times.

Not too long after the French Revolution had ended the traditional monarchy, Napoleon made himself emperor through his vast military planning and accomplishments. His campaigns led to Egypt and the discovery in 1799 of its ancient civilization. Artifacts and statuary were brought back, including the tablet later known as the Rosetta Stone from the place of its discovery. This key to the language of the Egyptians was incised with the same inscription in three languages. This allowed Champollion to decipher it in 1821, thereby giving the first understanding of hieroglyphics. The period also saw the first modern discovery of Pompeii and Herculaneum and their undisturbed art treasure. The Empire style, as it became known, included the ideals and motifs of these ancient civilizations, and was later called Neo-Classic. This is an illustration of how entire motifs were adopted and combined from disparate sources into one new creative style.

The Academy of Fine Arts, part of the Institute of France, was the ruling body of French painting and held an exhibit twice a year. The Classic style, with its emphasis on line and subordination of color, was the only one permissible for paintings shown there and it became static and lifeless due to its enforced repetition.

Some French painters began to defy the Academy openly, starting the Romantic movement. They used light, color and movement, creating emotional compositions that can be referred to for modern utilizations and arrangements. The subject matter was removed as far as possible from the proscribed classic myths and forms of the Academy. They included everyday subjects and reworked versions of the Medieval traditions of the crusades, and stories from Dante and Shakespeare.

In England, the Elizabethan period and the Age of Reason of the seventeenth century had followed their own course, and there were no corresponding Baroque or Rococo periods. But the Romantic Era had many of its roots there in the late eighteenth and early nineteenth

Western Art, Textiles—Embroidered, English, First half XVII Century. Panel. *The Metropolitan Museum of Art, Rogers Fund,* 1928

centuries. Painter John Constable developed Naturalism, the idea of working outdoors and painting nature's colors in a "multitude of greens." This marked the beginning of a new attitude toward painting and decoration that is still the source of many of today's compositions.

MODERN ART

France at the latter part of the nineteenth century was the scene of a revolution in art that was to have lasting world impact. The dominant theme was no longer the subject matter of traditional realistic representation, but instead the implied emotion of the artist's concepts. We owe much of our freedom of expression to these pioneers.

The works of the early Impressionists were painted with what has come to be called a "rainbow palette." They used un-mixed color without shadow or realism in interpretation. At first they were not well received. In the period after 1880, when the work of many of these artists gained recognition, Post-Impressionism was born. During this time, they began to use Symbolism and experiment with other approaches to painting. They started to manipulate the natural structure. In Symbolism, emotional content of more abstract thoughts and ideals were expressed with various shapes and forms.

Painters like Gauguin and Van Gogh used bright color and shape to impart emotions. The impact of their work was felt in the Fauvists and later Expressionists. Among the Fauve painters are Matisse, the acknowledged leader, Dufy, Rouault and Vlaminck. Their work is a study in how color can be used effectively in bright combinations. They were also among the first to appreciate the arts of Africa.

Cézanne was interested in spatial relationships and he began to move forms around to suit a composition. This eventually led to Cubism and hard geometric analytical works.

By the early 1900's other artists started to include many of the ideals of these works. Paintings became more abstract as they turned into experiences in themselves.

The Cubists used an understanding of planes to break up the surfaces of specific objects and paint them in a geometric way. Then they actually rearranged forms and put them together on canvas as they

Sketch from a Braque Ceramic

felt they should be, not as they were. Picasso, Braque and Duchamp are among the early Cubists. Later on, Cubism became totally abstract as artists selected elements of plane and mass, using them purely as they saw fit, within the background and space.

The Expressionists used space, color and form to express their own reality. Many of the artists were connected with the Bauhaus school and Expressionism is often felt to be a Central European movement, which included such artists as Paul Klee, Wassily Kandinsky and George Grosz, as well as Klimt and Munch. Kandinsky was the first to paint a pure abstract work with no recognizable objects early in this century, a landmark in Modern Art.

As the non-objective traditional took hold, the composition and design of paintings and other works was of utmost importance. Due to the lack of representational subject matter, they are often valuable

Right, John Hall, "Rainbow", 1971, ht. 25″, w. 15″, depth, 3″. *Photo: Studio, New York Times. Assemblage Construction Courtesy, Louis K. Meisel Gallery*

studies in design. The use of form, color, texture and space are other contributing factors of note.

Another group of artists, the Surrealists, specialized in the unexpected. They wanted to create a new sort of reality through the combination of usually unrelated ideas. Within the general term, there is representational Surrealism including actual objects as seen in the works of Rene Magritte, Marc Chagall, Salvador Dali and Giorgio de Chirico. Abstract Surrealism, with forms alone, is expressed by Joan Miro and Jean Arp and is an indication of how flexible and open to individual interpretation your designs can be.

Later in this century, the works of a group of artists in America came to be known as Abstract Expressionism. This is still an influence today and includes artists like Willem de Kooning, Arshile Gorky, Stuart Davis and Jackson Pollock.

Other schools of art combine to produce the artists of today, whose work is an expression of personal vision. The recent trends are becoming ever more diverse, as people begin to experiment in many areas, without feeling the need to be bound by any one school, or in some cases, any one medium.

An awareness of the historic background of the arts can certainly add to the very experience of seeing any work of art. Your own ideas may be changed by looking at a new form or type of expression that may have seemed strange at first.

Picasso, giant of our times, is particularly fascinating in this regard as his genius was such that almost every period or trend in Modern Art can be seen by studying his works in chronological order. As single works, they are equally impressive, as a growth series, they are amazing. Henry Moore is a sculptor whose works are of great interest in their organic form and mass. Studies in color and abstraction are seen in the works of such diverse artists as Mondrian, Matisse, Léger, Klee, Miro, Vasarely and Joseph Stella.

Such a variety of art works exist today that they are a study in contrast. Broaden your own vision by discovering in turn how others perceive and picture things.

CHAPTER SEVEN

The Arts Of The East

THE ARTS OF THE NEAR and Far East provide us with distinctive design outlooks quite different from our own. They developed in separate areas with a relative independence from the arts of the Western world. In both cases, we can find much beauty in traditions that are simultaneously different and challenging.

The arts of the countries of the Near East are generally classified as Islamic. This religious influence is a power from Morocco to India and includes the countries in between. The most important developments in the arts of Islam were in Mesopotamia (including Iraq), Asia Minor, Syria, Iran (once Persia), Egypt, Turkey, Spain—during the Moorish occupation of the Middle Ages—India and Afghanistan. Only in India is there another major influence, that of Buddhism.

Islamic art grew into the rich tradition starting from the seventh century. Their decoration was neither exclusively religious or secular, but rather an elaborate presence in everyday life, with the exception of figure representation, which was forbidden in holy places. The floors, walls and ceilings of their rooms were richly ornamented with design instead of being crowded with furniture. From the makers of these rugs, tiles and molded ceilings came masterpieces of creative pattern. Their work was stiictly regulated by guilds, maintaining the quality without stifling the development. Although there is a degree of variation between the various countries, the overall aspect is fairly unified and recognizable as such.

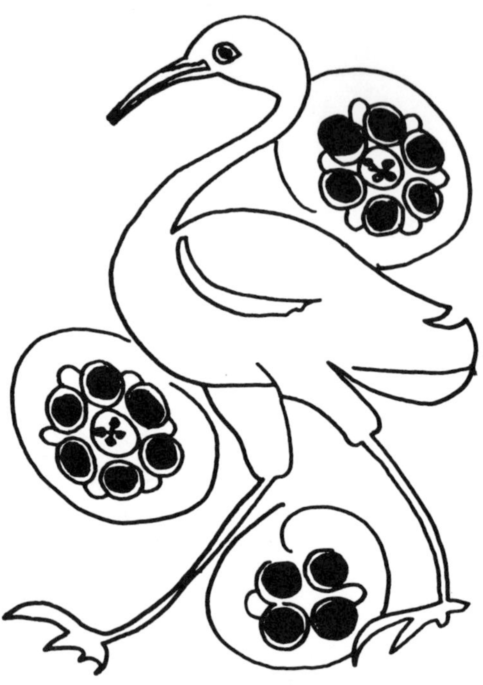

From a 15th Century Moorish plate

Moroccan Tilework

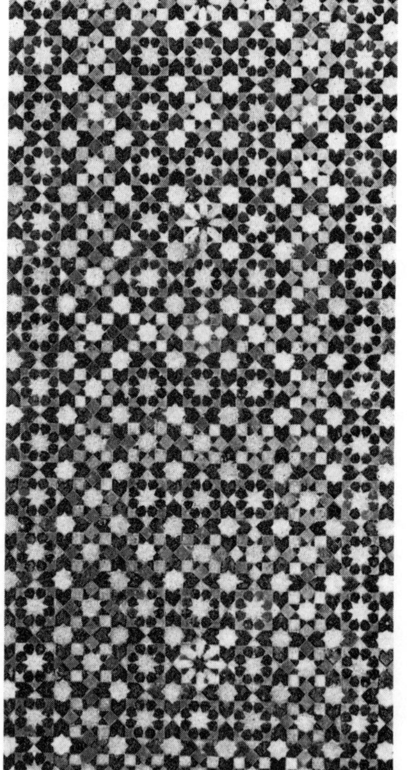

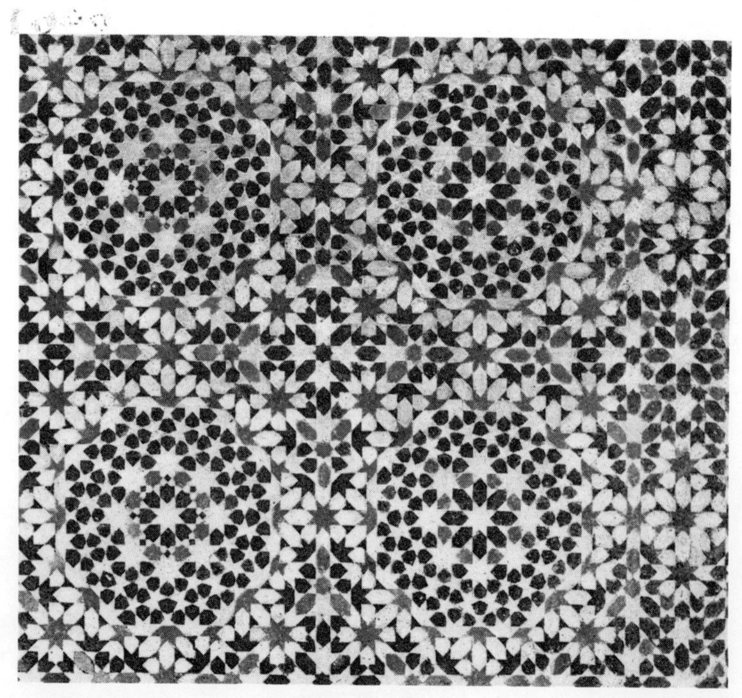

The details found in pottery, weaving, calligraphy, miniatures, bookbinding and metalwork provide us with a body of design possibilities that are exotic, exquisite and seemingly endless. The scope of the work includes the faithful renderings of Indian flora and fauna and the stylized flourishes and arabesques of Persian and Moorish representations of almost mythical looking creatures. The span of time of the classic objects available for study ranges from about the seventh century to the eighteenth and continues to a lesser extent up to the present. One of the most interesting areas to look into is the fine rug weaving. These rugs, often meant originally for prayer and a spot on the wall, never the floor, had symbolic patterns. The animals and flowers in Persian designs are done with a mastery of color. The colors also had significance and the rarest today are rugs containing green, as they were revered and few were made. For geometric and patterned weave designs, the Turkoman, Turkish and Caucasian are the rugs to seek out.

From a 13th Century Syrian plate

Islamic style borders

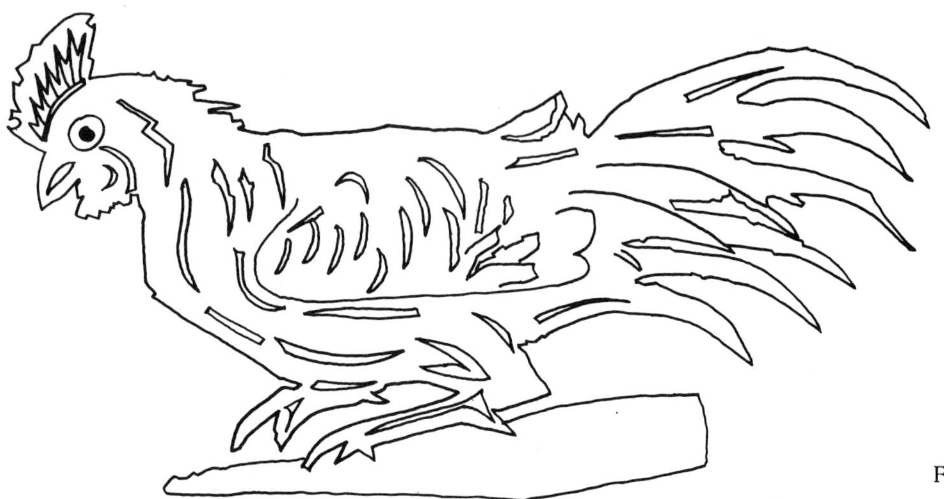

From a mosaic in Tunisia

The arts of the Far East developed on their own, with little or no contact with the outside world for centuries. China's recorded history began over three thousand years ago. The only real influence, outside of the period of Mongol rule in the fourteenth century, was Buddhism, introduced from India by travelling Chinese merchants about 2,000 years ago.

In the fine art of painting, the Chinese are greatly involved with line and delicate coloration. Paintings are done on screens, scrolls and wall panels. The strokes of a bamboo brush are the result of a lifetime of training. The strict tradition uses ink and brush on silk or paper, working from memory. There are no preliminary drawings and the changing of errors is forbidden, so that a controlled form is an essential ingredient.

Sculptures, porcelains and lacquerwork are finely planned and executed. The fine white kaolin clay was widely imitated once it was seen in the West in the fourteenth century, although the Europeans used white paint to emulate its qualities until the same type of clay was discovered in Europe centuries later.

China is also considered responsible for the introduction of block printing, fine weaving pattern techniques, paper, explosives, and porcelain made from the kaolin clay.

The Chinese Ming dynasty produced some of the most famous porcelains and works of art in history. The motifs employed have been included in many non-Oriental designs for their distinctive flavor and style.

During the seventh century, the Buddhist influence began to permeate the island nation of Japan. The prevailing arts of the native

Sketch of a porcelain lion

population were all but replaced by the Chinese modes. This influence was first brought indirectly through Korea and then by Chinese immigrants and Manchurian invaders.

Korea also transmitted other elements of the Chinese culture to Japan. The Koreans had in many ways remained more Chinese than China itself as they had adopted the Confucian religion and retained it long after China had become Buddhist. As Korean artists and scholars provided Japan with their own stylistic sources, they naturally conveyed the many areas that had been founded in the Chinese.

Korean potters had worked since before the Christian Era in the West and they continued a fine tradition, unique in itself while including other motifs.

The first records regarding Japan date from their fourth century invasion of Korea, but their own reckoning dates their first emperor

Covered Bowl, Punch'Ong, 15th Century Korean, early Yi dynasty, ht. 6″. *Collection, Mr. and Mrs. Gregory Henderson. Photo, Maia Henderson*

Fuji Musume, "Wisteria Maiden". 18th Century, 28″ x 11⅜″ color on paper. *The Cleveland Museum of Art, Anonymous Gift. Courtesy, The Asia Society*

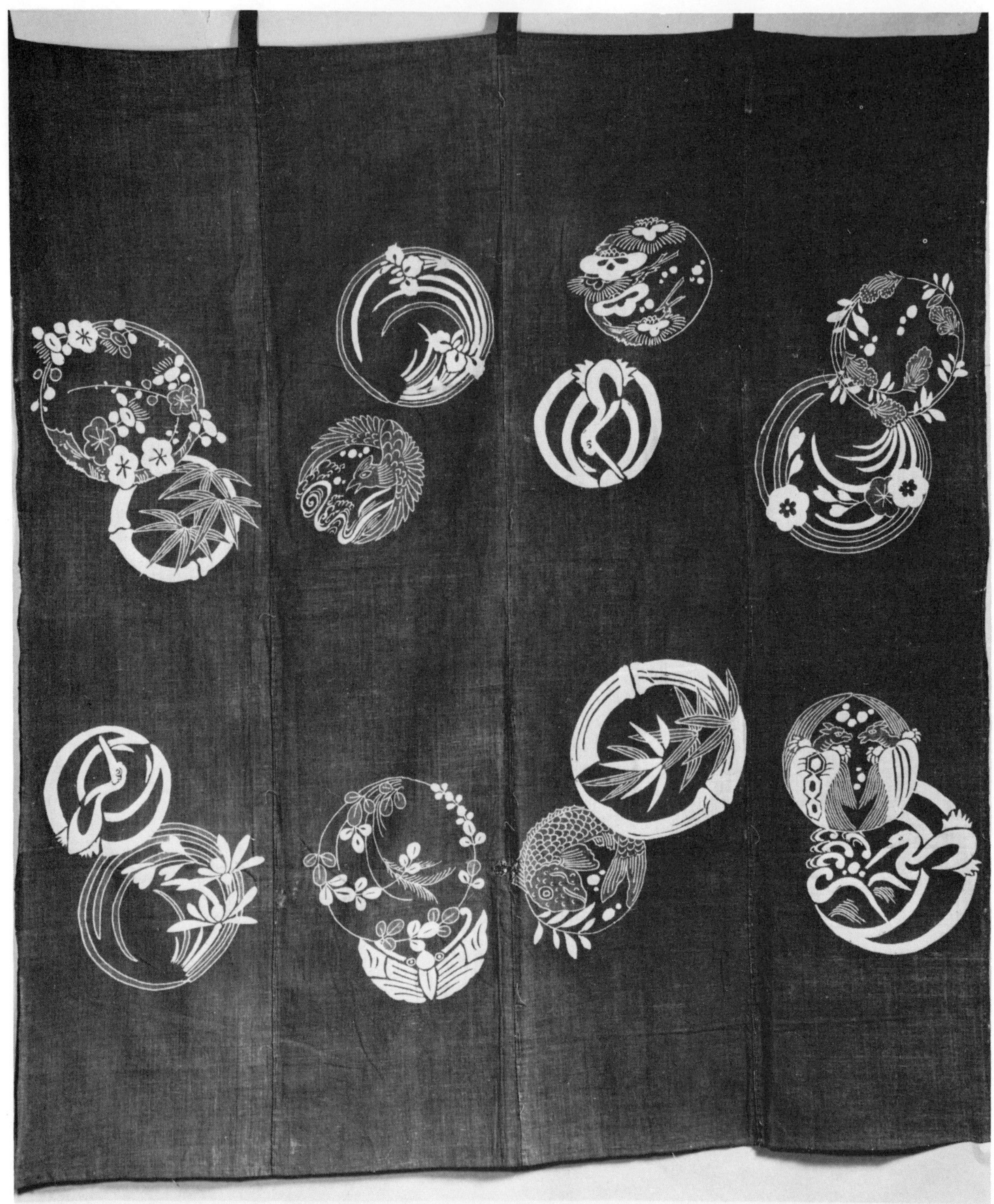

Futon Cover, 54½″ x 50″. *Japan Society.*
Courtesy, The Asia Society

at 660 B.C. The history as we know it starts in the seventh century when the ruling family adopted the Buddhist faith. Immediately after this period, the Japanese ceramics, painting and design follow the Chinese quite closely and then start to develop in their own way while maintaining an indirect relationship.

Japanese decorative arts, fine arts and architecture are based on a tradition of attention to the smallest detail, with a purity of motif. Strongly linear, nature is one of their favorite subjects, including lovely renderings of birds, flowers, other living creatures and landscapes. The colors are subtle and quietly worked.

Katsugi, Tohaku cotton dyed blue and green. *Japan Society. Courtesy, The Asia Society*

The influence of Japan on the decorative arts of our century is tremendous and their asymmetric prints were fascinating to many of the early Modern painters. Their lacquerwork, woodcarving, flower arrangement—Ikebana, paper folding—Origami, architecture and landscaping have also captured the imagination of the world, as seen in many a modern Western house.

The stylized figurative and abstract motifs are created with an excellent figure-ground relationship. Many Japanese patterns are printed in both negative and positive versions without impairing their effectiveness. The simple black and white designs for fabrics and papers that employ no color at all are most expressive. The study of this type of design is called Notan and you may wish to look into it further as a source of dramatic understatement.

Stoneware plate, Japan, Edo Period, Seto. 10½″. Grass, moon and geese design. *N. V. Hammer, New York City. Courtesy, The Asia Society*

CHAPTER EIGHT

Primitive and Folk Art

FOLK ARTISTS, ALTHOUGH LARGELY UNTRAINED in the usual sense, have an inherent appreciation of design and pattern. Their untutored approach lends freshness and charm to their work. Often the products of native or folk artists are abundantly decorated, in many cases with abstract, geometric and naturalistic motifs. These are an important source of design structure and inspiration as they contain much that can be adapted to our own way of life.

You can find a wealth of design material in the works of many countries. They are available to us in the form of actual art works, sold as such in galleries and exhibited in museums, such as the Museum of Primitive Art or the Museum of American Folk Art, both in New York City, to name just two of the many that exist in the United States. Magazines such as those published by the Museum of Natural History in New York City and the Smithsonian Institution in Washington, D.C. as well as National Geographic often show examples of works of this nature. There are also many books on the subject, covering the folk arts of the world, most often broken down into a single country, area or population group.

An invaluable source of American folk art style and technique is the Index of Design, a project prepared by the WPA during the Depression. It contains literally thousands of painted renditions of these arts and has been excerpted and printed in several books, although the originals are still in Washington, D.C.

As you look at these works, notice how many of them fall into recognizable categories, such as geometric, which is seen in and used by so many diverse civilizations. The abstractions of natural forms are often well suited to designs in craft media, as so many of them are actually executed in one such medium or another. Individual elements of design can be found within an overall larger design or included on their own for a complete pattern. You can see how the concept of a certain form is translated into design by examining these works with an eye toward discerning their source in nature, as so many are based on the artist's surroundings.

As we look at the works of folk artists it is usually easiest to track them down by country or group. A continent such as Africa contains so many separate cultures that they can best be examined one at a time. The artistic traditions are bold and strong, using various standards of work according to the area and cultural influence. From one end of the continent to the other we find numerous styles and motifs.

African culture was largely unknown and unexplored by Europeans until the end of the nineteenth century. Once discoveries were made of the richness of the continent, Europeans began to build vast colonial empires in pursuit of its many natural resources.

Three sketches of African Art

As the countries of Africa became independent, they continued and developed their own methods of expression. Thus, the traditions are carried on today, as the emerging nations retain their own identity and pride.

The African populations and their individual decorative themes can be roughly placed into groups by their general language and tribal attributes. The northern section of the continent is predominantly Hamitic and Semitic, the central and southern area is largely Bantu, the southwestern group are the Bushmen and in the west are the Sudanic peoples. Within these groupings are smaller tribes all with their own characteristics in art and design. Of course, there are similarities within the larger groups due to shared traditions. They are all concerned with fine design and skillful execution. Incorporated variations of the ornamental substance of their arts and crafts are evident in many areas and are frequently interpreted in popular Western wall papers, rugs, carvings and cloth as their rich tradition gains appreciation and recognition.

Native artists in other areas are an equally fine source of design possibilities. In the Western Hemisphere, the Indian cultures thrived in North and South America at various times and places, contributing their own unique styles and symbols to the lexicon of design.

The ancient Mayans lived in Mexico and parts of Central America and at their height produced refined works in pottery and sculpture, as well as writing and a calendar. The Old Empire collapsed in the eighth century A.D. and gave way to the Toltecs, a Central American group. They in turn were replaced by the Aztecs four hundred years later. Their stone carving and sculpture were intricate and richly textural.

In Peru, there were several early civilizations including the Chavin, Chimu and Nazca. Many were at their height by the beginning of the Christian Era in the West and created lovely decorative ceramics and metalwork. From their base at Cuzco, the Incans spread their influence over the entire area. Their textiles are well known and were created with abstract geometric forms that remain interesting. The powerful, organized Inca state lasted until the arrival of the Europeans, as did the Aztecs in Mexico. The changes that took place due to the abrupt outside influence were so vast that the entire Indian history before their arrival is delineated by the name Pre-Columbian.

All of these early civilizations share an understanding of well-planned design, characteristically in abstract or geometric style. They are still intriguing to today's designers due to the real quality and uniqueness of expression in their works.

The Indians of North America lived separately in various tribal groups throughout the land. Due to the general lack of contact be-

Sketch from an Aztec sun calendar

Sketch of an Aztec pectoral jewelry design

Opposite, Mask, Do, Upper Volta—Bobo, wood, paint, twine. ht. 72″. Courtesy, The *Museum of Primitive Art, New York, Gift of René d'Harnoncourt*

Sketch of a typical ceramic

Sampler, Peru—Nazca, cotton, wool 28½" x 42". *Courtesy of the Museum of Primitive Art, New York*

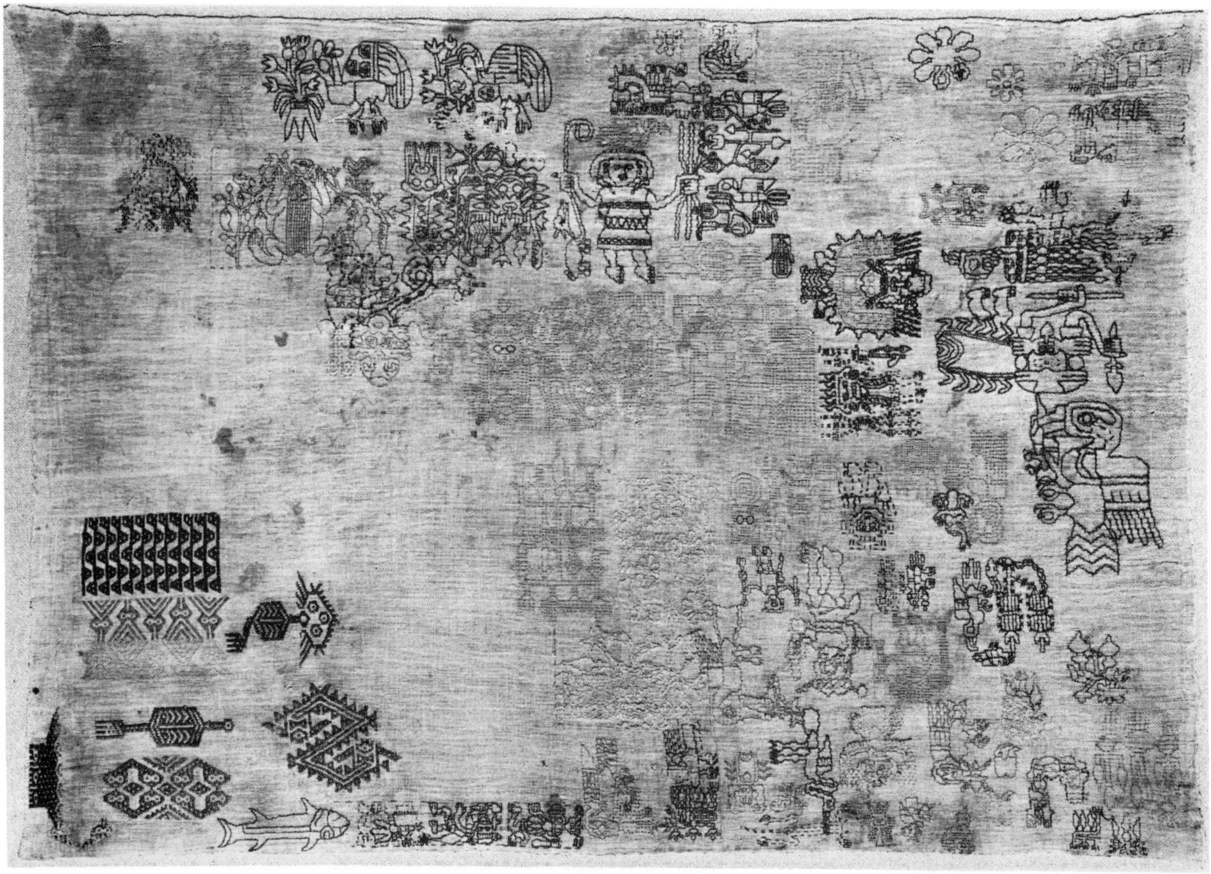

tween the groups, each developed a distinctive method of manufacture for pottery, weaving, basketry, leatherwork and beadwork. Their designs are likewise different, although they share the classification as abstract, geometric or symbolic. Almost all of the necessities of daily life were enhanced with design or pattern.

Although the Indians never discovered the potter's wheel, their ceramics are justly acclaimed. They have a truly Indian origin and style. The smoothed surfaces of pots, bowls and vases are decorated with designs applied by hand-made leaf brushes and colored with vegetable or mineral pigments. The black and white patterns are also very effective. Other types include black or red ware with incised or raised design areas. The choice of technique and pattern is dependent on the tribal group. As the modern descendants continue these traditions, they blend the old and new together with fine results.

Photos on pages 103-111, courtesy of U.S. Department of the Interior, Indian Arts and Crafts Board.

The ancient craft of basketry also continues to be a major source of expression. The techniques are handed down from generation to generation, retaining their distinctive design vocabulary. Natural reeds, plants and fibers gathered by the basket's maker are used to both construct and color the baskets. These hand-woven patterns show

Mary A. Histia, Acoma Pueblo, Jar, c. 1967, earthenware, slip painted, ht. 8¾″

Margaret Tafoya, Santa Clara Pueblo, Jar, 1969, earthenware, burnished black oxidized finish with sunken relief decoration, ht. 17⅞″

Margaret Saraficia, Papago, basket, 1964, Yucca coiled, 17⅜″

how the method of manufacture can influence the design as each motif fits into the limitations of this kind of weaving.

Quillwork demands hours of laborious preparation of porcupine quills into small tube-like beads, which are then fashioned into patterns on clothing, footwear and other apparel. Sometimes the introduction of glass beads by traders in the last century replaced quills.

Sophie New Holy, Sioux, man's breast plate, 1964, porcupine quills on rawhide, 15¾″

Nettie Standing, Kiowa, Necklace, 1964, glass beads, 30⅞″

The Navajo squash blossom necklace is an example of how several elements can come together and become the mark of a certain group. The central pendant, known as a naja, is thought to have come from the Moors as introduced into Spain during their occupation during the Middle Ages. As the Spanish rule was forced onto the Mexican Indians, they learned the trades and their artisans spread them to the

Necklace, Navajo, c. 1955, Silver, 31″

north, including many of the motifs. The metal work became popular with the northern tribes, some of whom had previously mined turquoise by hand, using it for beads.

As they began to work in metal crafts, each group developed characteristic methods and styles. Native Americans of today still create works in silver and stone. Navajo silverwork is generally quite heavy,

Bracelet, Navajo, 1969, Silver, 2⅞″

Irene Bea, Navajo, Wall Hanging, 1964,
Wool, 25½″ x 36″

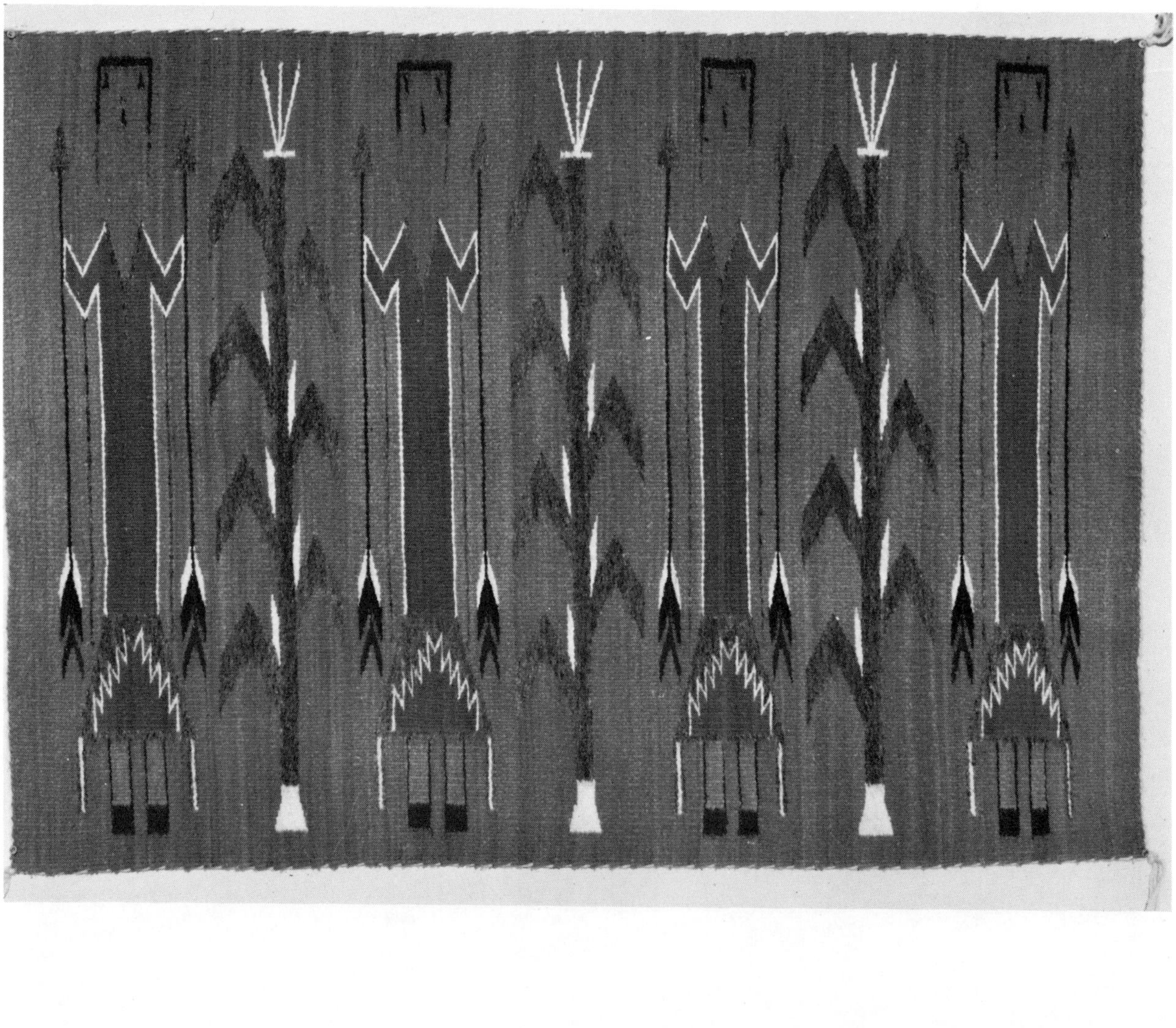

Pin, Hopi Pueblo, 1969, Silver Overlay with oxidation, 2⅜″

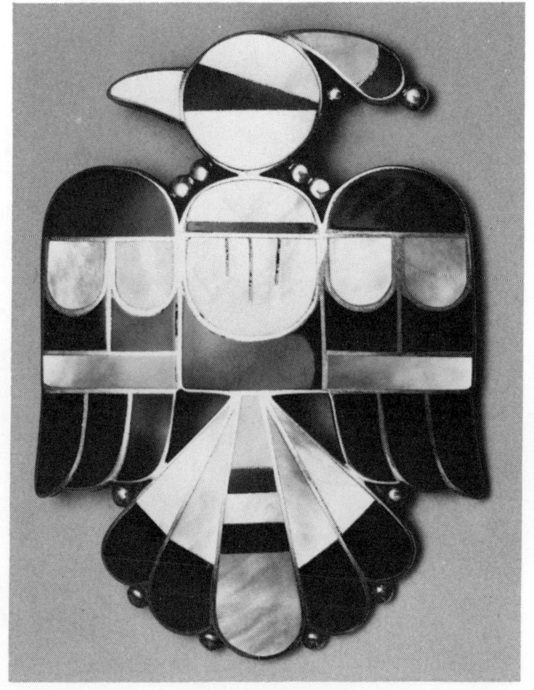

Myra Tuscon, Zuni Pueblo, Pin, 1968, Silver with inlays of shell and jet, 3″

with a great deal of silver and few stones. They are also known for their hand-spun, hand-made woven blankets and rugs. The ceremonial or yei blankets have patterns taken from the traditional sand paintings.

Hopi silversmiths are known for their overlay method, which welds two layers of the metal to each other so that the carefully cut out design in one layer looks like a textural carving. Their patterns are adapted from their unusual pottery designs. The Zuni do wonderful settings for stones, placing small fragments together in inlay and channel techniques, so that they create a sort of stone patchwork, with the silver being subordinated.

On the Northwest coast of America, the Tlingit and Haida tribes are particularly skilled in woodcarving and stencil work. The stencil patterns had an original symbolic meaning, as each small section stood for a certain object. These stencils and carvings are quite decorative in their rounded rectangular forms.

Still farther north, Eskimos carve fine works in the native stone, as wood can be relatively rare. Their subjects are taken from the environment and most often include the animals that populate the near arctic cold, and were so essential to survival. The sculptures are somewhat abstract, but highly expressive. They show motion and the inherent sense of the animals' simple but meaningful stance.

Alexander Akeya, Eskimo, "Bears Attacking a Walrus", 1964. Soapstone, 8″

Left, Lincoln Wallace, Tlingit, "The Strong Man", 1966. Yellow cedar, carved and painted, ht. $55\frac{1}{8}$″

In so many cases, the lesson that can be learned from the folk arts of such diverse civilizations is the beauty of unsophisticated expression and technique. The works are both highly decorative and timeless.

In the search for fascinating pattern and abstract design, we can look from Africa to the South Seas and back without ever covering the ground completely. In all lands, native and folk design is abundant and its strengths have influenced many a modern artist.

Left, Tapa cloth, Polynesia, Fiji Islands. Tapa, pigment, 7′8¼″ x 9′1¾″. *Courtesy of The Museum of Primitive Art, New York, Gift of René d'Harnoncourt*

Shield, Melanesia, Solomon Islands. Basketry, mother of pearl, clay and paint, ht. 33¼″. *Courtesy of the Museum of Primitive Art, New York*

CHAPTER NINE

The Decorative Arts

THE DECORATIVE ARTS SURROUND US, in home and office. They are the articles used every day, including furniture, metal wares, textiles, ceramics and other accessories. As such, their relationship to the people and times that produce them is unique. As the products of artists, working in fields other than the fine arts per se, they embody the style of our times.

These arts quite often have applied designs that are of interest in their own right and can be inspirational to you because they are expressive of the period that created them. They also encompass an incredible number of designs, due to the sheer volume of articles required by the public. The continual demand stimulated, for example, the production of fabrics in numerous colors, textures and patterns.

Within the variety of selection, we can discover motifs and patterns, creating new design ideas. All branches of the decorative arts are equally fruitful. They have been made in all places, periods and styles, including examples throughout history. These arts are so essential to everyday pleasure and comfort that they can be seen everywhere we look. Museum exhibits, gallery displays, antique stores and fairs, fine furniture and department stores, all provide us with many sources of new concepts in style and design. They offer a wealth of material that can be successfully interpreted into other media.

The world we live in is populated with all types of preconceived designs. Even the simplest objects are the result of hours of trial and error, search and research. All of the life experiences of a designer come to bear upon the ultimate design of an object. The final rendering is the result of a mental process that is enhanced by the knowledge of what has been done before and where the need arises for new conceptions of old forms.

Everyday objects like these are chosen for their usefulness as well as their beauty. They can be evocative of other forms in themselves and you should keep an eye out for interesting shapes, swirls and masses of color that are suggestive of other ideas and designs. Try to look at familiar articles as if their use was unknown. Notice the texture, hue, planes and forms of the things that surround you. For a wider vocabulary of design information, learn to react to them in new ways.

An increased awareness of the abundance of shapes and forms will add to your repertory of ideas. When designing a free form or abstraction, call the known shapes to mind. From there, you can proceed to think of variations. It is essential that the variety of idea forms you can recall be as wide as possible.

In studying objects that have additional interest in surface design enrichment, your background in motifs, designs and patterns will naturally increase. These objects are just as useful to you as a designer as learning to see designs in unexpected places and are easier to notice, too. The design of all things wrought by human hand, or by nature, is well worth a second look.

As the planned functional design of an object is interrelated with its decorative design, the tendency to think of an applied design as just that should not be mistaken for the facts. Only a design conceived together with, and as a part of, the functional aspects is really harmonious with them. However, a good functional design often ends up with a charm all its own, even without any ornament. A suspension bridge is designed for ultimate strength and durability, with the most economical use of materials. Yet, out of this plan develops a graceful beauty.

As we see from past history, what is thought to be beautiful in one age is not always regarded as such in later years. But the idea of timelessness is one of the standards by which we often judge the relics of the past. This is due to the natural evolution of design in historic terms. When the realistic use of shading was unknown, there was no way to develop a design that incorporated a strong feeling of three dimensional weight and mass. Other aspects of design were then utilized. As the use of realistic shading became widespread, there was room for development in other areas.

With the coming of the Industrial Age, many designs for the products of machinery were made to imitate hand-wrought forms. These types of design were not suited to their new uses and something had to be done. That solution wasn't completely found until the twentieth century, when furniture and other necessities of life found new shapes, that were well formed by machine and were specifically designed that way.

Long before then, the struggle for quality design in the decorative arts was often marked by the dichotomy between good taste and ease of production. Out of that problem arose several movements that advocated good design and fine workmanship. The seeming lack of artistic merits in the productive Victorian Era in nineteenth-century England stimulated the formation of the first of these movements.

In 1848, the Pre-Raphaelite Brotherhood was founded by a group of English artists. They espoused a return to the simpler days of the Medieval period before the High Renaissance and the painter Raphael, as implied by their name. They resented the ornate Victorian style and the increasing encroachment of machines on quality work. Their aim was to become more familiar with nature and to bring back finely wrought forms. They included such people as Dante Gabriel Rossetti, Ford Madox Brown, and William Morris. They made use of Medieval

Stained Glass window by Rosetti

"Peacock and Dragon" woven wool by William Morris. *Courtesy, William Morris Gallery*

motifs for much of their work, including a sort of mysticism that had its roots in the period, preferring the severity of Gothic style.

As a member of the Brotherhood, William Morris, a designer, scholar and craftsman, advocated the pleasure and dignity found in hand-crafted work. His growing convictions of their worth led him to found the Arts and Crafts Movement. Through it, he expressed a desire for both a return to natural form and a rebirth of fine quality in the decorative arts. He designed patterns for fabrics and wall papers that are still popular today. He worked in many areas, including weaving, embroidery, and the founding of a publishing house, Kelmscott Press. The bindings and pages of his books were beautiful and elaborate, often using the two type faces he developed for use there.

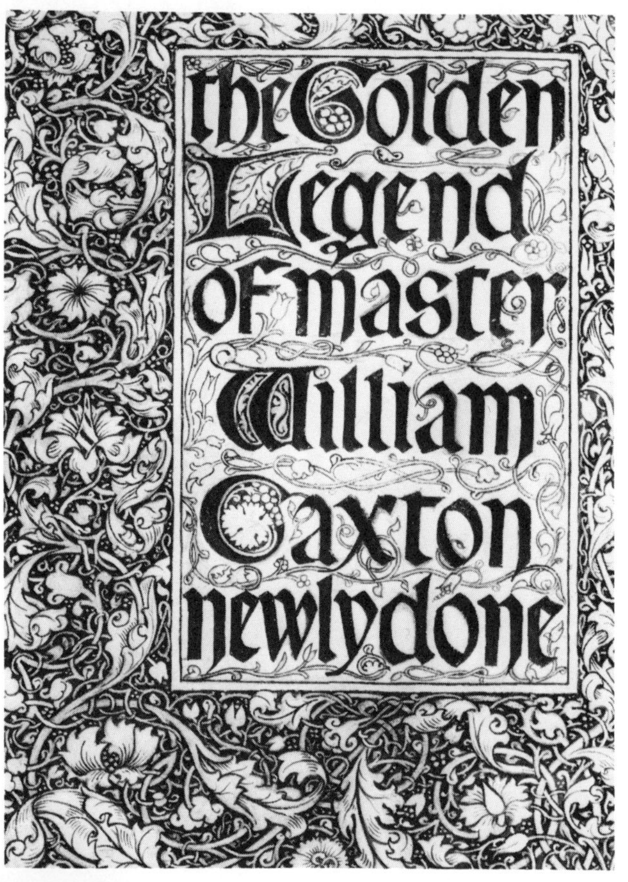
the Golden Legend of master William Caxton newly done

"Golden Legend" Kelmscott Press (title page)

"Love is Enough" binding by William Morris

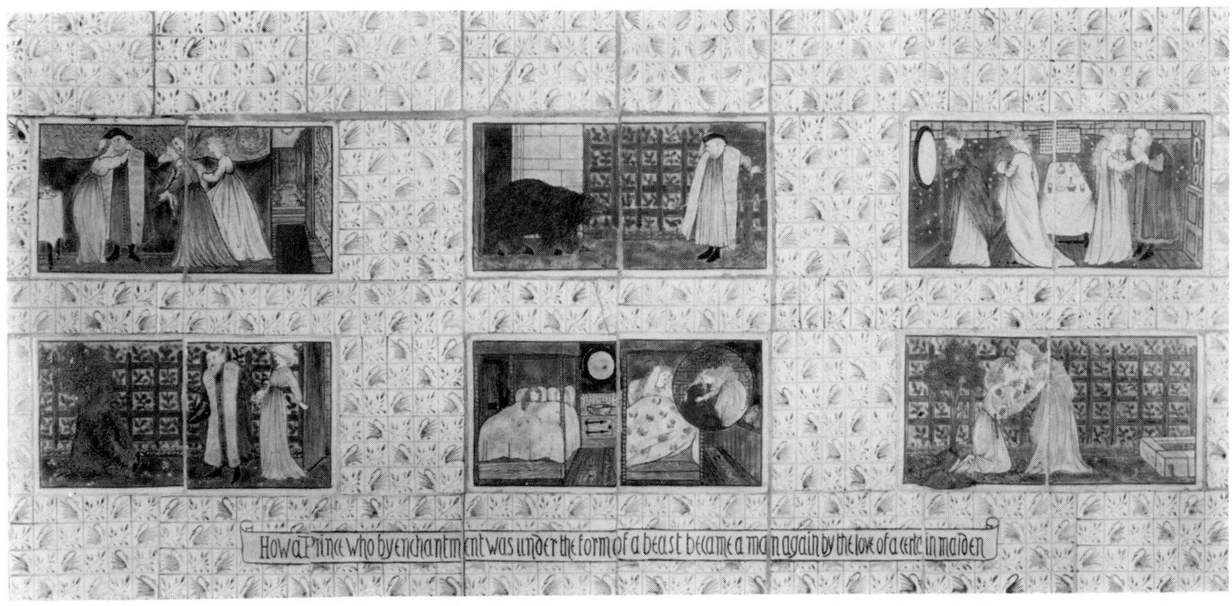

Ceramic tile panel "Beauty and the Beast" by Burne-Jones *Courtesy, William Morris Gallery*

"Thorns and Butterflies" cretonne by Mackmurdo *Courtesy, William Morris Gallery*

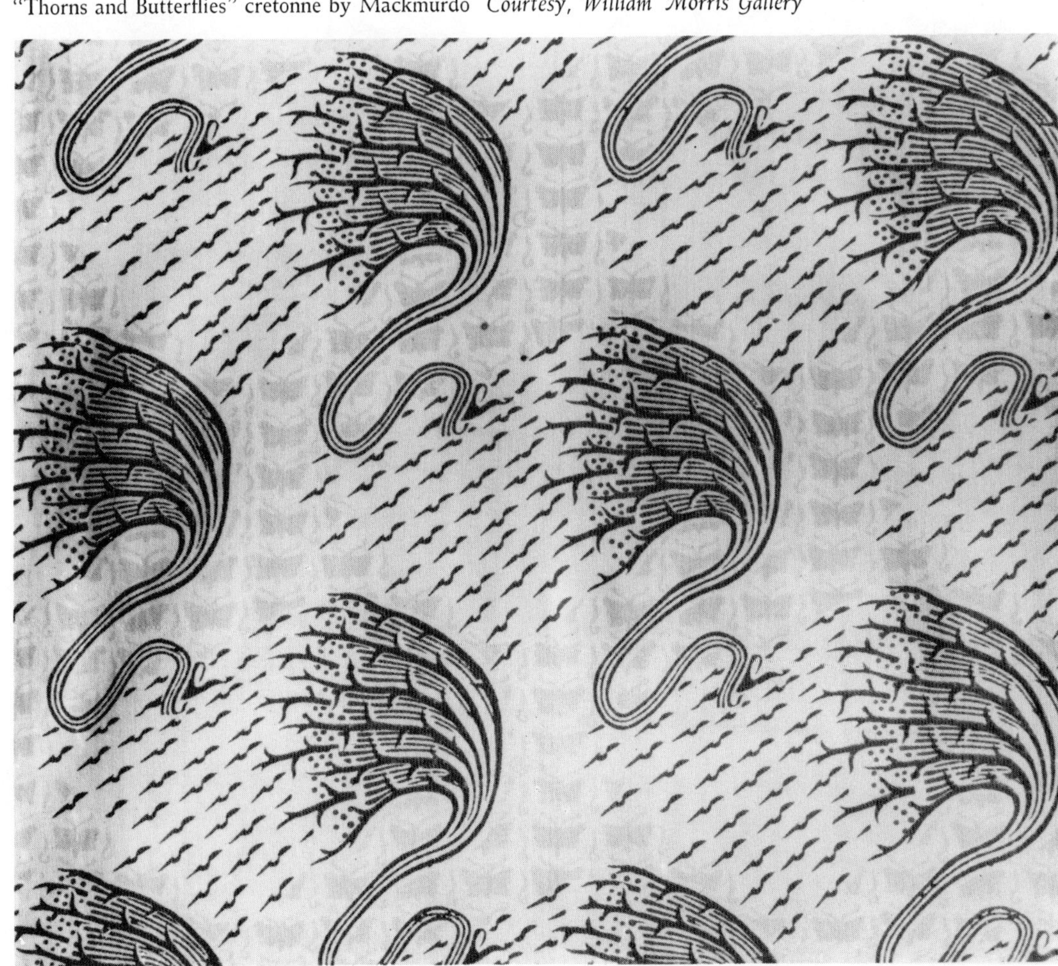

Drawing Room at 1 Holland Park,
William Morris Decoration
Courtesy, William Morris Gallery

The Morris movement covered all areas of home furnishings—fabric, wall paper, furniture, pottery and ceramics, metal work and stained glass. Among the artists who worked with him were Burne-Jones and Mackmurdo. Their work makes use of Medieval themes, Biblical and mythical scenes and allegories, as well as subjects from nature. The natural forms are among the most interesting—attractive birds, flowers and animals.

In America, the Arts and Crafts Movement was best known for the art potteries that were founded and flourished around the turn of this century. They created many advancements in glazes and decoration that are in demand today as antiques. The Rookwood Pottery in Cincinnati was the first, founded by a woman in 1880. They were innovative in their use of underpainting, particularly of flowers and leaves, and at their height employed some of the best designers of the day. Other potteries of a slightly later date include the William H. Grueby Pottery in Boston, which was the first to produce the distinctive dull, matte finish glaze, and the Van Briggle Pottery in Colorado.

Rookwood vase

Other furnishings were made following many of the ideals of the Morris movement and later of the movement itself in America. It was never as much of a cohesive unit as the English Arts and Crafts Movement, being a rather loosely related group of people who believed in fine design and well-made products.

Perhaps the most famous American associated with the movement was Frank Lloyd Wright. As an architect, he designed furniture and other objects to go into the houses he planned. His later work was in a different vein, but his appreciation of good work and the natural form of the environment is always apparent.

The Arts and Crafts Movement in the United States enjoyed a moderate success during the first decade of this century as it promoted the ideals of quality. This influence was felt for many years even though the style itself might have changed. Many examples of the work show an increasing development of the aspects of functional design in the fabrication of objects used every day, without a repetitive imitation of older forms. The exponents of the movement were pretty much dispersed by the time of World War I, but their impact remained.

One of the stylistic sources of the Arts and Crafts Movement was Art Nouveau. Literally meaning New Art in French, the style was sinuous and organic. It actually flourished in Central Europe more than in France, but the name adhered. It was also known as De Stijl and Jugenstil. It started toward the end of the nineteenth century and continued into the twentieth. Its most distinctive characteristic is the use of flowing line and natural forms. The depiction of flowers, leaves and branches is easily recognizable.

Art Nouveau's influences are seen in the fine arts and architecture as well as in furniture, jewelry and fabrics, which were well suited to

Art Nouveau Silver Jewelry

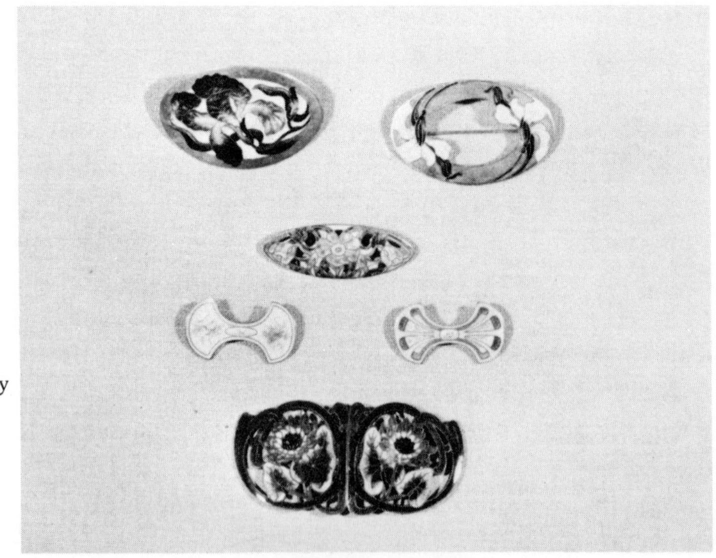

Art Nouveau Enamel and silver jewelry

Japanese fabric stencil, Edo Period, 13¾″ x 5¾″, Cutout paper. *Japan Society, New York. Courtesy, The Asia Society*

its languid line and movement. Some of the roots of the style are found in the Japanese decorative arts that became so widely known in the late 1800's and the Pre-Raphaelites. Among the fine artists of this period who were involved in Art Nouveau were Central European painters like Edvard Munch, Gustav Klimt and Ferdinand Hodler, who is often thought to be the first to use it seriously. Other examples of Art Nouveau are the fine posters of Frenchman Alphonse Mucha and, of a slightly different nature, Toulouse-Lautrec, and the somewhat decadent book and magazine illustrations of Aubrey Beardsley in England. These have all recently enjoyed a revival and their smooth curves and shapes lend themselves quite well to many forms of craft interpretation.

In the United States, the Art Nouveau period is exemplified by the work of Louis Comfort Tiffany. As an artist, his work in glass is known for its use of scintillating color. He designed intricate leaded glass lamps and windows with the natural forms of plants and insects broken down into small segments of sparkling hue, but unified in design. His iridescent glassware was partially inspired by the ancient glazes on Egyptian and other Near Eastern ceramics of antiquity, but it was unique. Many of the formulas were known only to him and have never been duplicated.

In 1919 in Germany, architect Walter Gropius became the director of the Bauhaus, a school of design. It was to develop into one of the major influences on the style of our times in many areas, including painting, typography, photography and poster design.

As applied to industrial products, the style of the Bauhaus began to change the look of modern homes. It stressed new design for machine products that were both functional and attractively well made. Although Hitler closed the school in the thirties, its teachers and students spread the ideals and orientation to the corners of the globe.

Alphonse Mucha poster
Collection: Sandra Ley

Handbag. Beads embroidered on suede. U.S. Department of the Interior, Indian Arts and Crafts Board.

Bracelet, by a craftsman from Hopi Pueblo. Silver overlay, with oxidation. U.S. Department of the Interior, Indian Arts and Crafts Board.

Transitional Art Nouveau-Art Deco pitcher.

New forms, complementary to their productive sources were made by people like Mies Van Der Rohe, who worked in America after the forced closing of the Bauhaus school. The Barcelona chair, designed by him in 1929, is a modern form that is timeless. It is used in decorating schemes today as much as it was when it first appeared, if not more so. The firm but pliant leather seat looks inviting while the sleek lines are adaptable to any modern setting.

The need for such good design is obvious, and is appreciated in our society with the well deserved recognition of current designers. They have made the first real break with tradition in such a long time that their work is an achievement.

As few people can afford hand-crafted chairs at today's prices, they should not have to settle for inferior design in mass-produced machine-made products. A fine example of the suitability of machine-made forms for excellent design is the molded furniture of Charles Eames. Its early use of plywood, and later plastics, was revolutionary. Eames' furniture has a continuing influence on the things we buy today as well as continuing in popularity themselves.

Lucite is an example of a material that was misused for a long time. The benefits of synthetics, like plastics and man-made fibers, in a world of limited resources are unquestionable. Yet at first they were made only to emulate natural organic materials. Used in that way, they offered nothing special and could be considered as imitations at best. But used in designs that enhance their own unique qualities, they have a beauty of their own.

Art Deco was a style applied to the decorative arts whose name is a contraction of the popular Arts Décoratifs exhibition held in Paris in the twenties. The prevailing curved lines of Art Nouveau became hard corners and stepped geometrics as Art Deco caught on in Europe and America. Its sources include the non-objective geometric paintings of the Bauhaus school, the newly rediscovered glories of ancient Egypt, American Indian art and Art Nouveau.

Art Nouveau floral

Dominating the decorative arts in the nineteen twenties and thirties, fabric, metalware, ceramics, jewelry and then architecture all became Art Deco. A revival of interest in the style has produced instant antiques, some as little as forty years old. There has also been an increased use in contemporary decorative pieces, with the echoing of shapes that is so distinctive.

A further aspect of the decorative arts is how they are arranged in a setting. When you furnish a room, you make a design that will be lived in. The components of the design are combined following the same general guidelines regarding proportion, scale, balance, texture and color as any design.

The style of furnishings we choose is indicative of our lifestyles. One

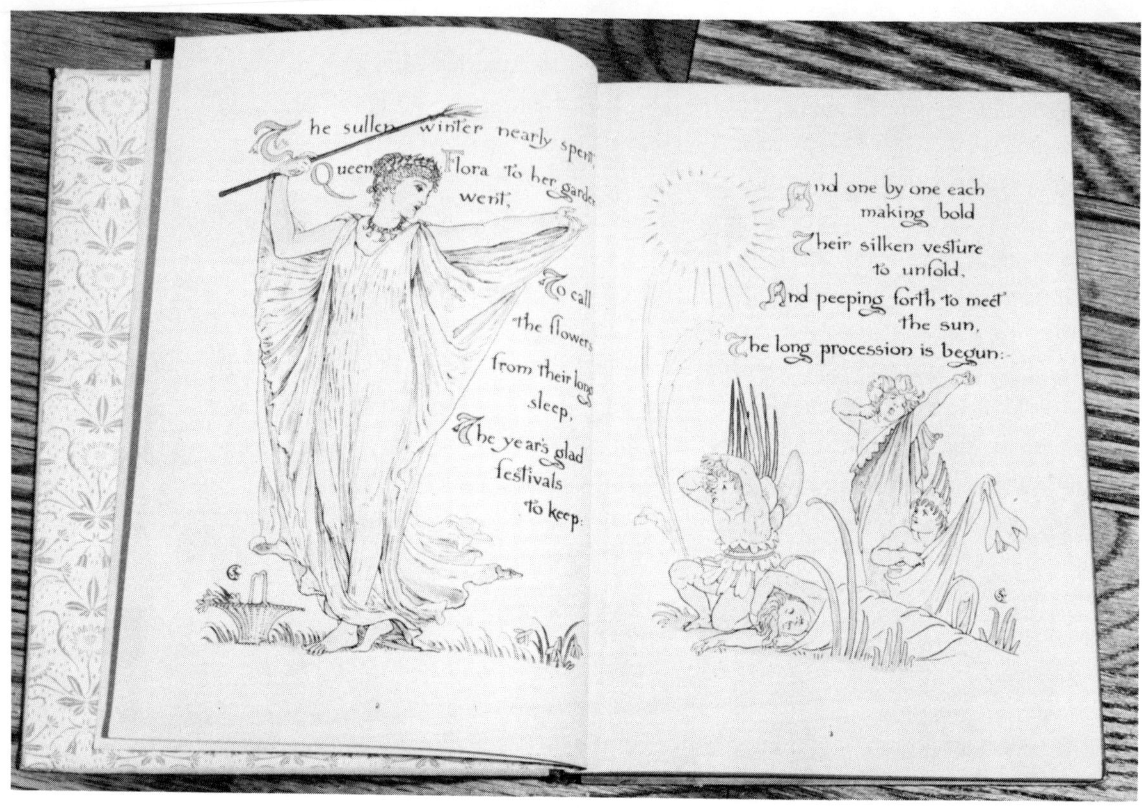
The sullen winter nearly spent,
Queen Flora to her garden went,
To call
the flowers
from their long
sleep,
The year's glad
festivals
to keep:
And one by one each
making bold
Their silken vesture
to unfold,
And peeping forth to meet
the sun,
The long procession is begun:

And Love's own flower the blushing Rose,
The Queen of all the garden close:
And Roses from the hedgerow wild,
Behind their thorns that faintly smiled.

Left, Pages from "Flora's Feast A Masque of Flowers", "Penned and Pictured by Walter Crane", published by Cassell & Co., London, 1899. Collection: Sandra Ley

Louis Comfort Tiffany iridescent vase

Art Deco jewelry

person may feel that the most important part of their surroundings is comfort, while another may prefer serviceability and quick clean-ups, while a third might enjoy the formal beauty of period rooms.

The way your house is furnished naturally says a lot about you, reflecting the kind of objects that you have chosen to see every day. In that way they can be crucial to the style and direction of the articles you will plan to make to go into any room, as they become part of the larger design.

Today there is a growing preference for eclecticism, the mixing of periods and styles, in the selection of furnishings and related art work. The sleek forms of a purely modern room may produce a feeling of unease, as the very things that make it modern make it seem impersonal. On the other hand, this is often the kind of surrounding that seems most right for our times. This may explain why contemporary rooms are often a blend of periods and locales. The individual pieces can come from all over and still be combined to make a coherent,

Right, Nigerian Figure with collection of Navajo jewelry and Venetian trade beads.

Left, Three Moroccan vases, Chinese Buddha, Indian Bronze, surrounded by Philippine Baskets. Interior Design: Bob Patino Associates, Inc.

attractive whole. In the forefront of this manner of mixed furnishings is the inclusion of hand-wrought forms, crafted by peoples of all times and cultures. They are a human touch, a reaction to and a complement of the more severe modernistic elements. As an expression of this idea, we can perhaps understand why so many of us are finding pleasure in the creation of beautiful craft forms, which add variety and interest to any setting.

African figure, Nigerian, Indian marble pot and assorted shells.
Interior Design: Bob Patino Associates, Inc.

CHAPTER TEN

The World Around Us

THE NATURAL ENVIRONMENT HAS PROBABLY been the most widely-used source of artistic ideas, ever since the earliest people tried their hand at decorating their surroundings with pictures drawn on the walls. The depiction of nature is one of the most continuous progressions in the history of expression as evidenced by the subject matter of art through the ages. The inclination to represent the things that live and grow upon the earth is ever present. Flowers and plants have been reproduced in thread, paint, wood and stone in thousands of ways, ranging from the detailed realism of a botanical print to the fast blur of an abstraction.

The growth patterns and natural forms present in nature are of endless interest. The rings on a tree, the geometric spiral of a sea shell, the veins in a group of pebbles all have a simple beauty and sense of order. They are an infinite source of design inspiration. As things grow following the principles of symmetry, we can perhaps understand why people are so comfortable with designs in formal balance, with two matched sides, such as hands and feet.

Snowflakes are constructed with an exquisite geometric perfection that is never duplicated. The concepts of radiation and symmetry are shown by them. Similarly, the crystalline forms of many minerals have a shape and pattern of hard edges that are mathematically precise. The fossilized plants and living creatures that were alive so many thousands of years ago have their own qualities of fine natural design.

Trees

Pine nuts

Geranium leaf

Sunflower sketch

Sunflower. Photo: Olga Ley

The living creatures of today are yet another source of design concepts. The varied coloration of fur and feather are of textural note. While looking at the whole, consider the parts; the rich spotted coat of a leopard, the detail of intricate pattern on an insect's wing, the scintillating hues of a bird's plumage.

The whole of a landscape is another favorite subject. It generates a quality of restful repose that is naturally suited to design, both abstract and realistic. As you look at a natural scene with all of its complex parts, pay attention to each. Notice how the distant areas seem mistier and cooler in color, while closer up, things seem sharp and clear.

The variety of design in the natural environment is there to be seen. Yet, you may find that a drawing or other rendering will be less difficult to work with than trying to make an original sketch from nature itself. Many fine prints, photographs and other reproductions are available for study; they will allow you to view a flower or other living being in an already simplified or otherwise changed version. The hardest part—moving from three dimensions to two without losing the essential qualities—will already be taken care of and you can concentrate on the possibilities of design and pattern included in the work.

You will find that other things that surround you in your personal environment are fine subjects for representational craft ideas. These include renditions of pets—yours or that of a friend for whom you are making a gift. Here again, you will probably find it better to work from a photograph than to try to draw the pet from life. Other topics can include the equipment and accessories of favorite pastimes, such as tennis racquets, nautical flags, maps and other gear, or the bright flies and fishing rods. Similarly, the emblems and mottoes of fraternal organizations, schools or other clubs can personalize a design.

Just as Pop Art celebrated our times by using the items in daily use in new ways, you can literally see design everywhere you look, enhancing your repertory of ideas. The observant eye can pick up concepts from all sorts of things, by discerning their most interesting features. Everywhere you go, gather sensory impressions. The uneven pattern of aged brickwork could be a stepping stone to a design. The structure and other ornament of architecture can often be a source of pattern ideas, in the fine characteristics of buildings in cities and towns. The carved details on churches and temples built in the more traditional styles have always been of rich textural quality and offer ideas and motifs.

Each generation seems to find expression in a different sort of building. For an idea relating to a certain period, study the structures and interiors to get a feeling of how things really were at the time in question. Certainly the small sturdy rooms of Colonial days are in sharp contrast to the organic designs for living so prevalent today.

Flowers

Renie B. Adams, "Potted Cactus Basket." Cactus and sand lift off, there is a hidden basket compartment in the cactus. Crocheted cotton, ht. 8″. *Courtesy, Artist*

Left, Fabric stencil. Japan, Edo Period, 13½″ x 8″, Cutout paper. *Collection, Japan Society, New York. Courtesy, The Asia Society*

Antique Botanical print

C. & W. Endicott Lith. New. York.

ARCTOSTAPHYLOS PUNGENS.

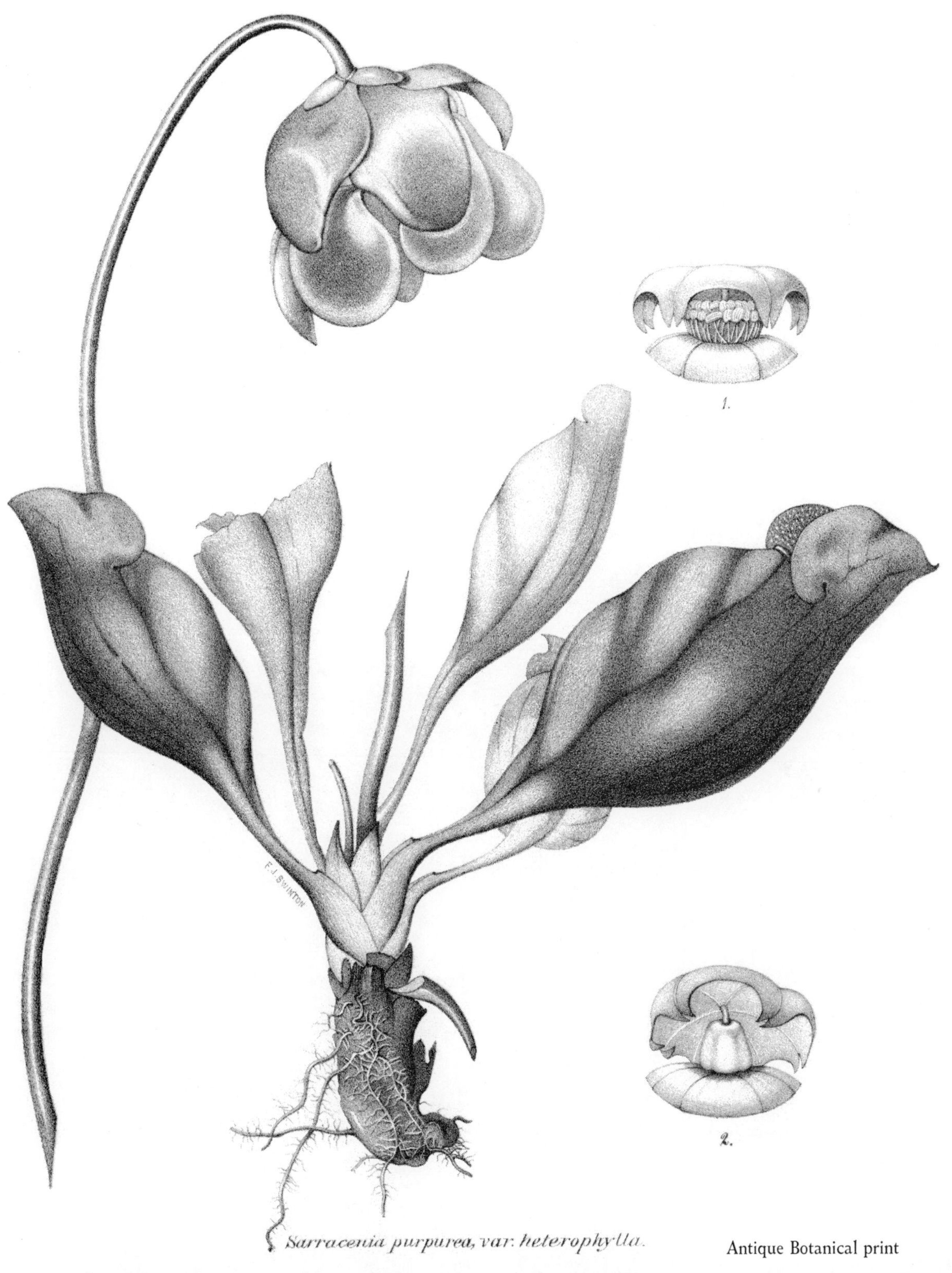

Antique Botanical print

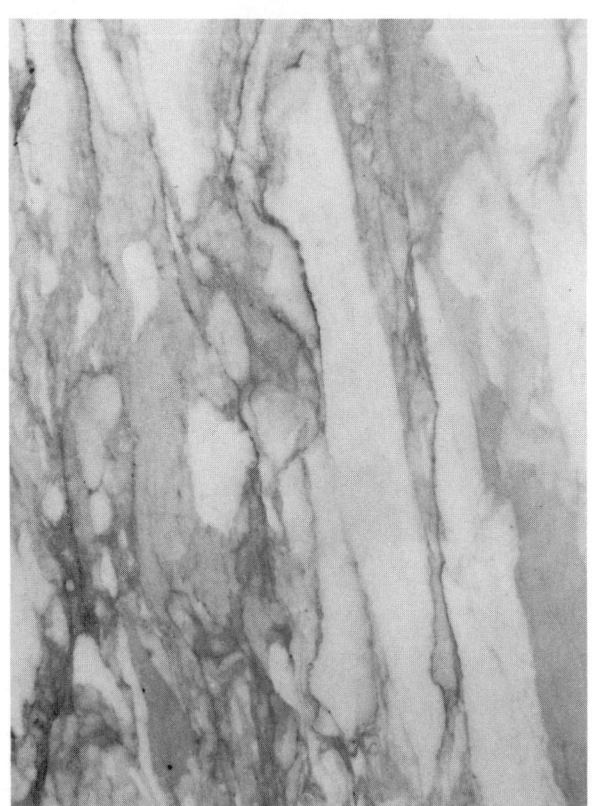

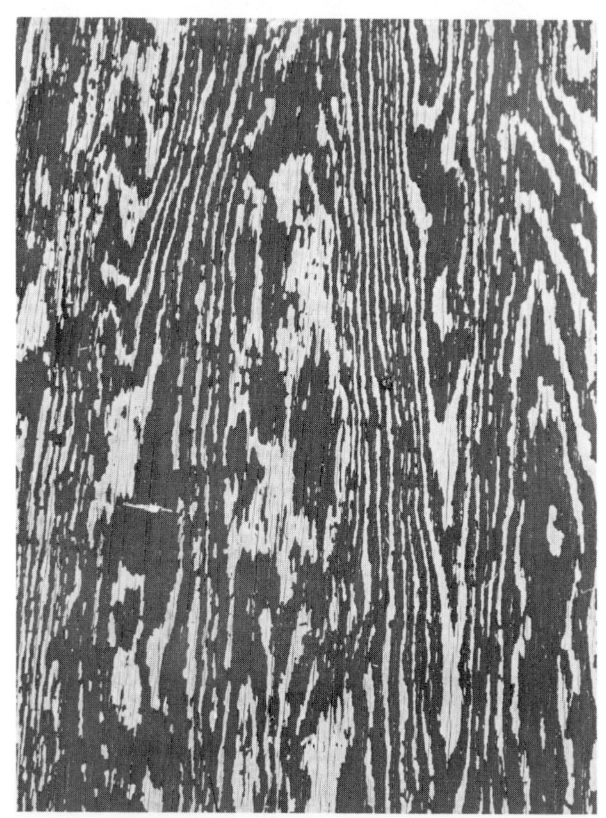

To make a visual record that can be consulted later on, you may enjoy taking photographs. The time that might elapse between sight and design can change the image in your mind. If you have a photograph, then you will have two impressions to work with. Any camera is useful for this kind of photograph, and if you become really interested, you might get a good camera and even consider printing the photographs yourself.

Photographs can be studied in other ways. Notice the smallest part as well as the total concept. Look at pictures you have taken of anything. A pattern of light on a building or a textural compostion formed by the sand on the beach may emerge. A snapshot you took on vacation last year might contain intricate sculptural details of the mon-

Left, Rhythms

Patricia Campbell, "Coral", crochet, linen, wool, nylon, 3′ x 3′.
Courtesy, Artist

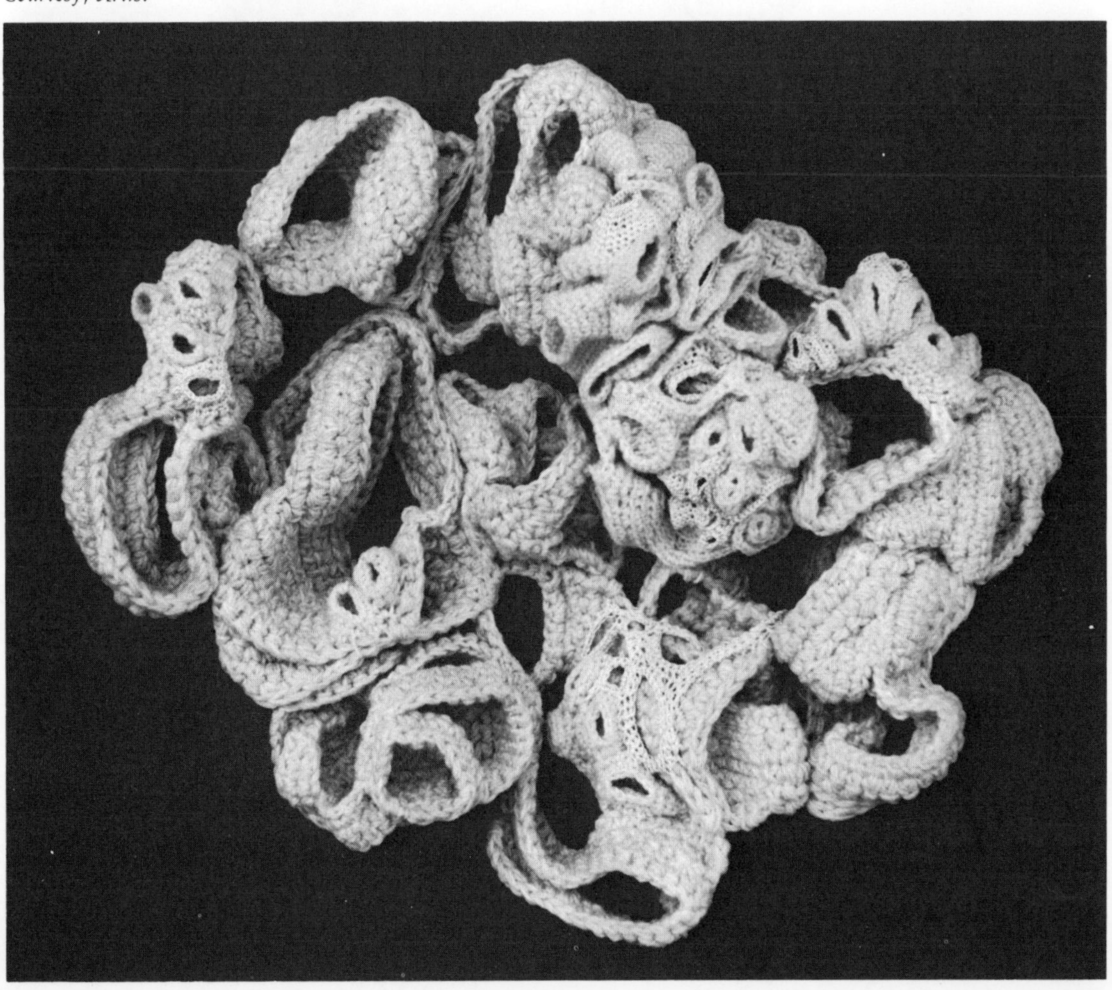

ument you were photographing, or the village scene might have a wealth of shape variation. It is a good way to look at familiar items and can be applied to photographs of all kinds.

It is also true that when you see a picture of a familiar scene that was taken by someone else, their conception of it may change your perspective as well. Conversely, if you had three people choose the section of a photograph that they would enlarge, you would most likely end up with three very different looking enlargements, just from the change in viewpoint.

As you go about your everyday activities, begin to really notice the design elements in the things that surround you. When you go to the city, note the contrasts in tempo, texture and pattern. Or, if you live in a city, learn to seek out the design in the country's more obvious charms. Each has its own excitement to offer.

All in all, you will be amazed at the rich variety of design and pattern insight and inspiration you will find just by looking around you with a view toward discovery.

Left, By a craftsman from Zuni Pueblo, figurine, "Owls" c. 1965, earthenware, slip painted, ht. 11″. *Courtesy, U.S. Dept. of the Interior, Indian Arts and Crafts Board*

Wood Owls. *Courtesy, The Appalachian Regional Commission*

Outdoors

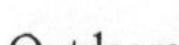

Outdoors

Left, Margaret B. Windeknecht, Hanging Rug, 32″ x 72″, woven black wool rya knots with an underlay of white. The inspiration for this piece was a neighbor's dog as the artist attempted to capture the sense of layer-on-layer in his coat, adding black beads through the central portion. Shown in Cooperstown, N.Y. show, 1972. *Courtesy, Artist*

Right, Mary Ann Scherr, Gold and Silver music box. Air/body sensor. Electronic device triggers music, "Smoke Gets in Your Eyes". *Courtesy, Artist*

Outdoors

Outdoors

Kay Whitcomb, "Positano", three-way switch plate, enamel on copper, chemical crust. *Courtesy, Artist*

Functional beauty. *Photo: Scott Chase Parker*

Chains and straw

Natural Composition in the sand

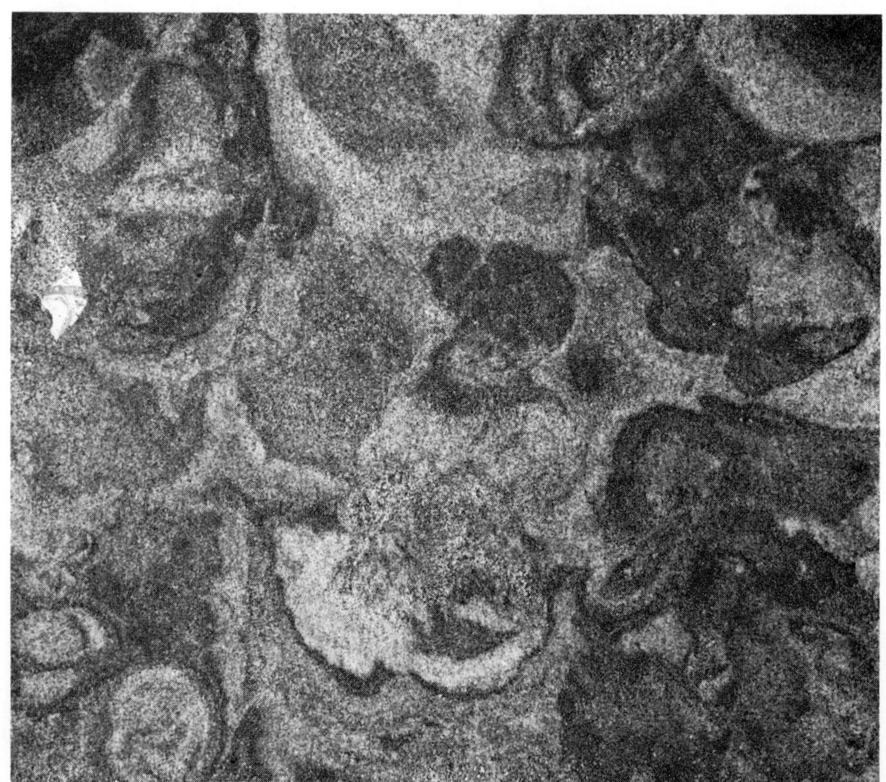

CHAPTER ELEVEN

The Artist's Workshop

TODAY'S CREATIVE CRAFTSPEOPLE ARE AMONG the most innovative and exciting in their forms of self expression. They have adopted and adapted techniques in many areas, finding new avenues of accomplishment.

The work of each individual artist provides us with a chance to view a piece of the world as seen and interpreted by someone else.

The choice of medium, method and style are all a part of the whole. The talents and materials come together to produce delightful results.

The visual selections are best explored and not explained, by looking. The subtle nuances in meaning in style and design are of importance to us and are there to be studied and appreciated.

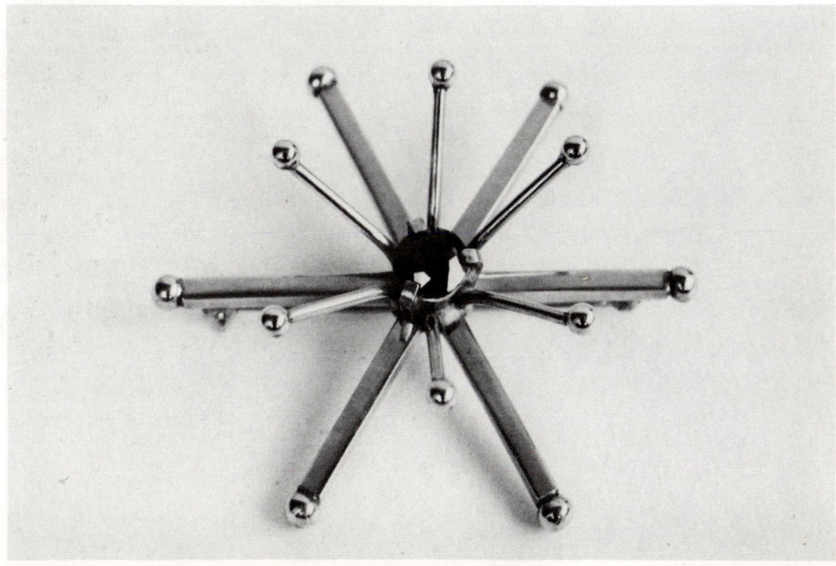

Margaret Sussman. Pin, 14 carat gold and garnet, 2″. *Courtesy, Artist*

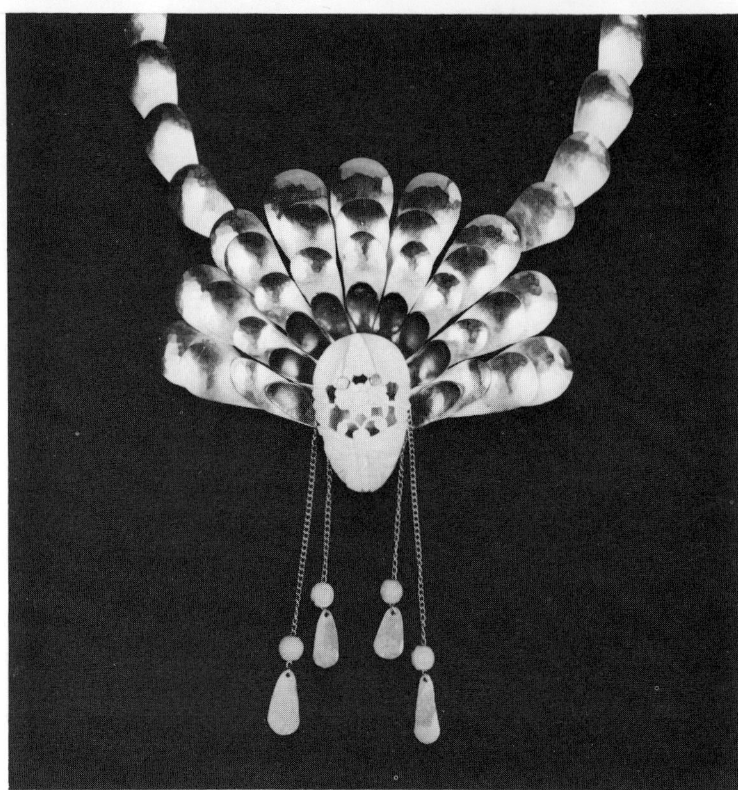

Left, Arline M. Fisch. Pectoral, "Peacock and Dragon Fly", silver and antique ivory. *Courtesy, Artist*

Right, Katherine L. Breydert. "Pietá". Embroidery. *Photo: Soichi Sunami. Courtesy, Artist*

Below, June Schwarcz. Electroplated foil. *Collection, Minnesota Museum of Art. Courtesy, Artist*

Right, Joseph Almyda. "Myth", 8′ x 6′, Batik, linen, with machine stitchery. *Collection, Fairmont Hotel, Dallas, Texas. Courtesy, Artist*

Kay Whitcomb. "Firebird", 1969, 26″ x 30″, enamel on steel. *Courtesy, Artist*

Right, Bobbi Beck. Stitchery

Renie B. Adams. "Circular Ceremonial Cloth". Crocheted cotton diam. 40". *Courtesy, Artist*

Right, D. J. Holmes. "The Lady and the Lion", 5′8″, white pine, polychromed. Carved in the style of a ship's figurehead of about the middle 1800's. *Courtesy, Artist*

Jean Stamsta. Untitled wall hanging, tubular weave, hand-dyed wool and synthetics, purple, orange and magenta, 48″ x 54″. *Courtesy, Artist*

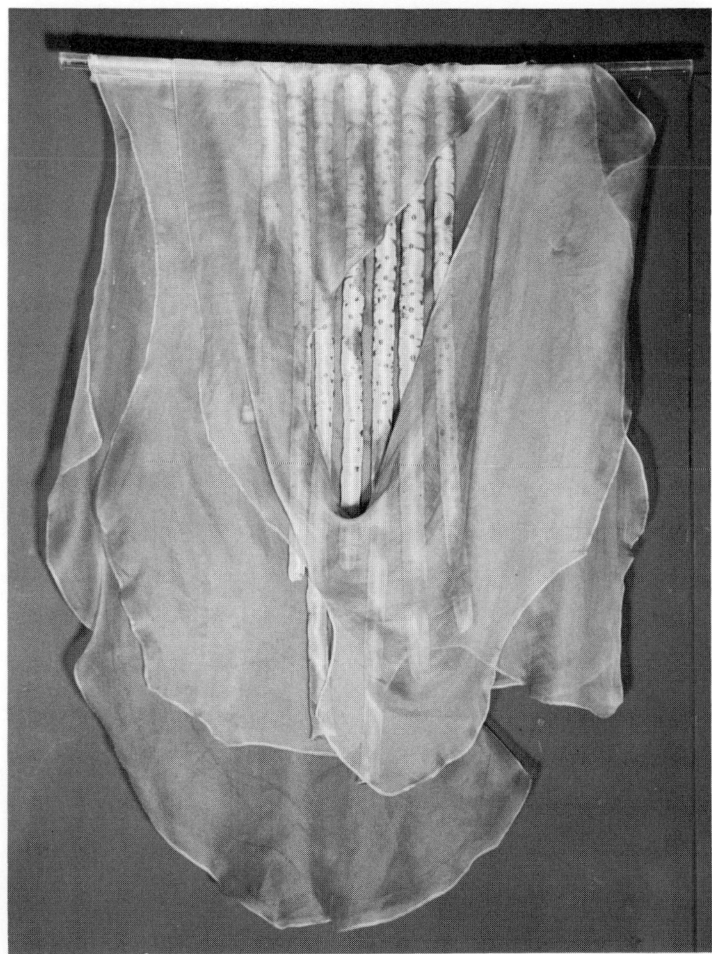

Kiyomi Iwata. Chiffon hanging with stitchery and stuffing

Margaret B. Windeknecht, "African Vibrations", macramé combining wool yarn, camel hair and stoneware beads. Inspired by a carved design on an African comb. In the Southern Tier Show, Corning, N.Y., 1973. *Courtesy, Artist*

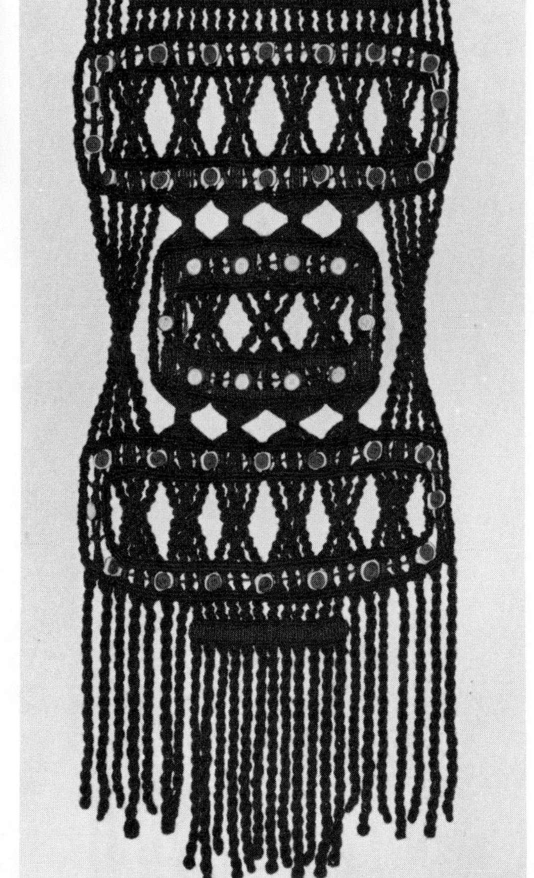

Left, Patricia Campbell. "Mask", raffia crochet, 2′ x 7′. Honorable Mention, Fall River Annual Show. *Courtesy, Artist*

Opposite, Yvonne Palmer Bobrowicz. Room divider, with brass elements as fringe to weight piece, 6′ x 8′. *Courtesy, Artist*

Mary Ann Scherr. Pulse sensor bracelet, open. First compartment amplifies and exhibits heart beat rate, picked up off pulse, through light emitting diode. Second compartment contains a sound system that alerts wearer when heart beat is erratic. Third compartment contains medication. *Courtesy, Artist*

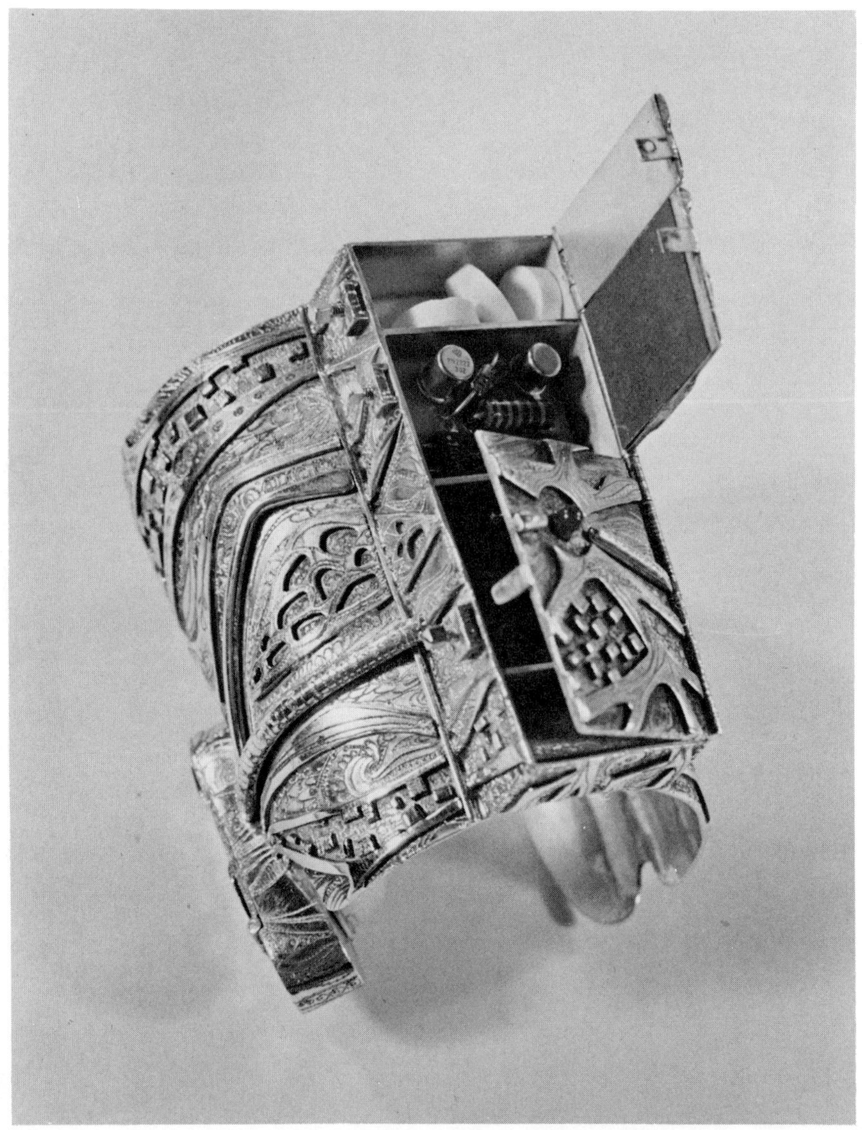

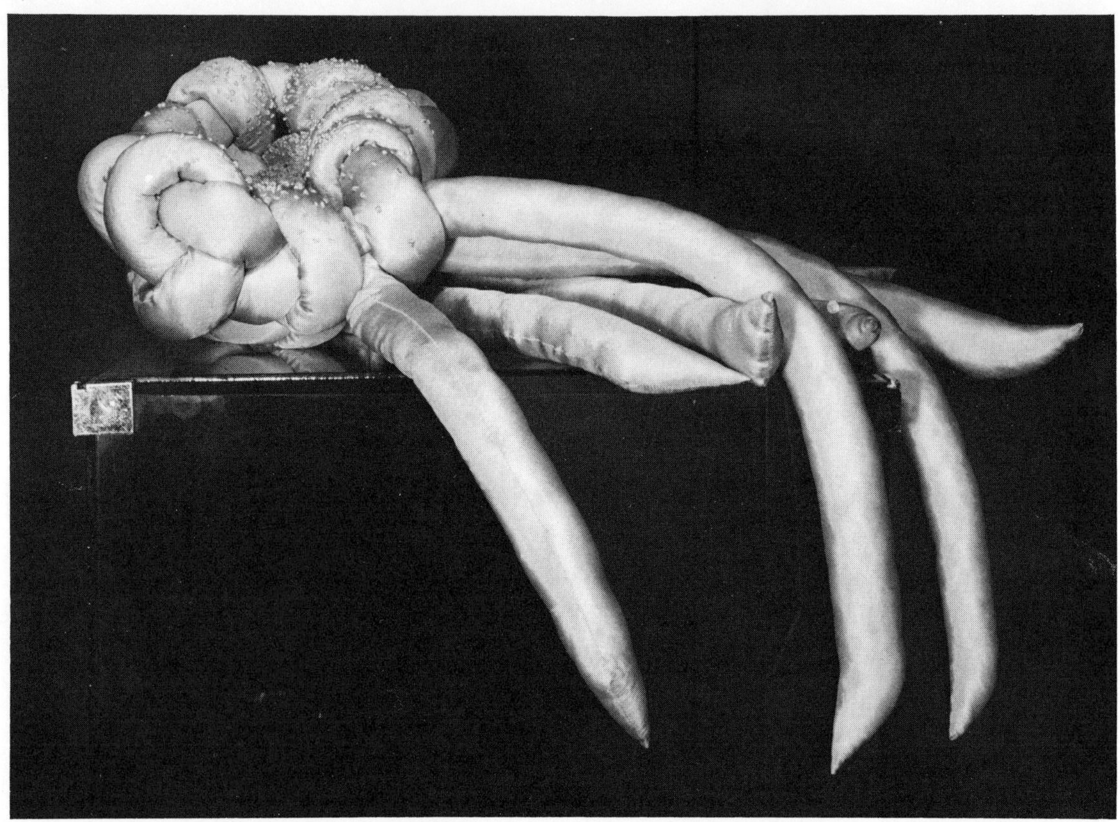

Kiyomi Iwata. Stuffed, knotted forms with stitchery.

Right, Jean Stamsta. "Small Power", woven, hand-dyed wool and synthetics, woven sculpture, 1970, 5′, black, white and gold, used to work out "The Three Powers", which were in the Fifth International Biennal of Tapestry, Lausanne. *Courtesy, Artist*

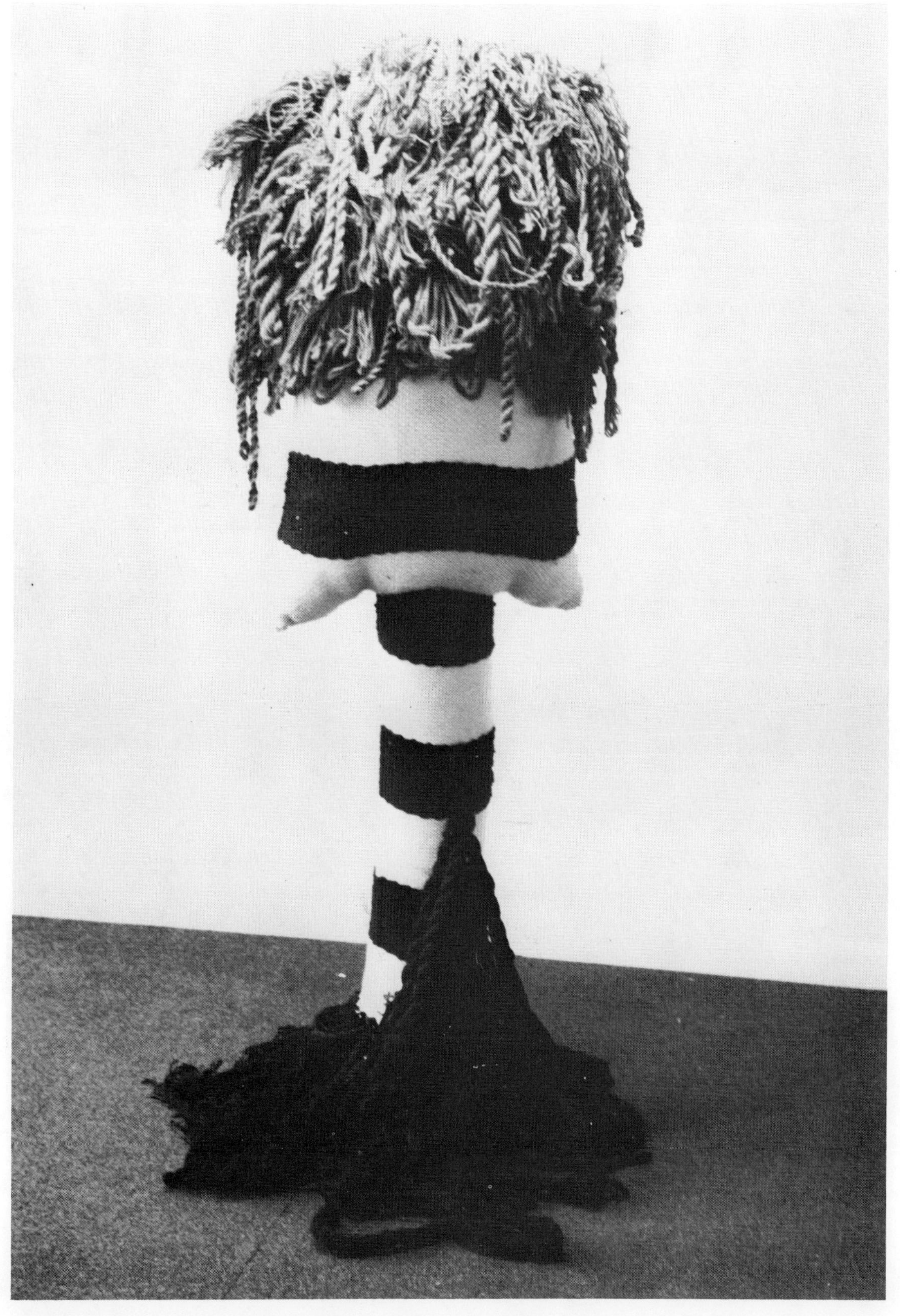

Joan Hall. "Sometimes I Stands and Thinks and Sometimes I Just Stands", 1973, ht. 16¾″, w. 15″, depth 4″. *Assemblage Construction, Courtesy, Louis K. Meisel Gallery*

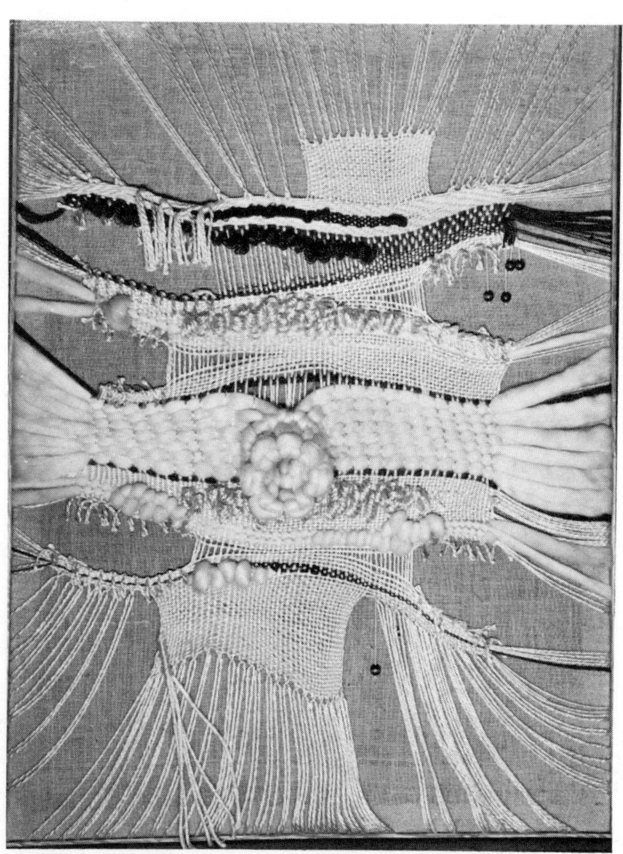

Paul Ratajczak, Woven study

Bobbi Beck. Stitchery

Left, Mary Nez, Wool rug, Navaho, 1965, 37½" x 60¾".
U.S. Dept. of the Interior, Indian Arts and Crafts Board

Jean Stamsta. "Oblio's Outpost", free standing sculptural weaving, approximately 5′ x 5′, hand woven of hand dyed wool, synthetics and dyed turkey wing feathers, black white, orange, red, purple; Untitled wall hanging, 18″ x 30″, hand woven of hand-dyed wool and synthetics with dyed turkey wing feathers, tublar weave and wrapping, red, magenta, black and white. Owned by Mr. and Mrs. Bill Brown, Penland, North Carolina. *Milwaukee Journal Photo.* Courtesy, *Artist*

Margaret B. Windeknecht. Batik on linen, 24″ x 36″, yellow, green, orange and brown, padding added for additional surface interest. *Courtesy, Artist*

Margaret B. Windeknecht. Batik on linen, 22″ x 72″, blue, green, rust and black, quilted.

Fannie Nampeyo. Jar, Hopi Pueblo, 1964, earthenware, ht. 4⅜″.
U.S. Dept. of the Interior. Indian Arts and Crafts Board

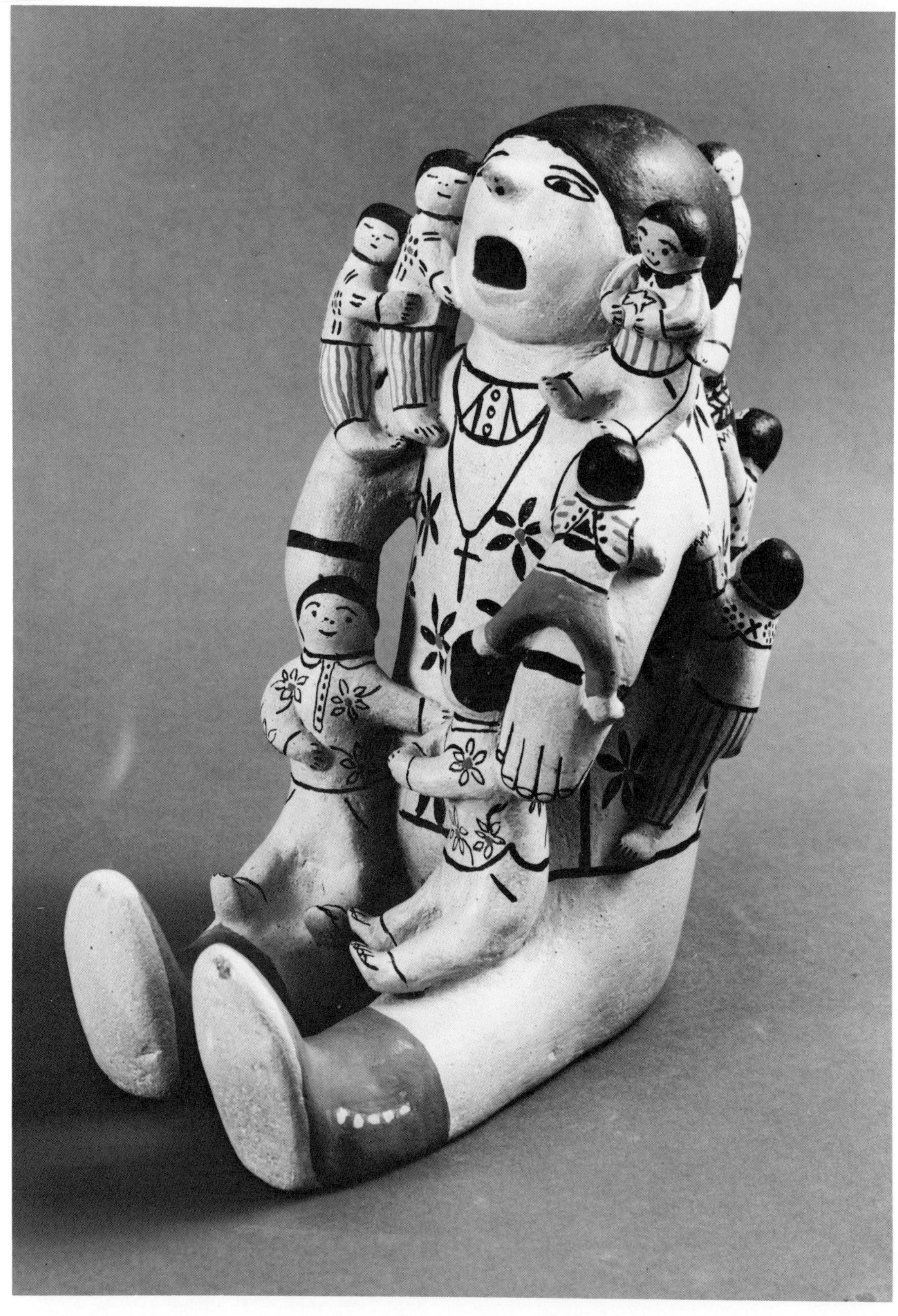

Left, Helen Cordero. "Storyteller", Cochiti Pueblo, earthenware, ht. 10⅝″.
U.S. Dept. of the Interior, Indian Arts and Crafts Board

Jar, Santo Domingo Pueblo, 1963, earthenware, ht. 8″.
U.S. Dept. of the Interior, Indian Arts and Crafts Board

Peter Seeganna. "Hunter", Eskimo, ivory on stone base, 5½".
U.S. Dept. of the Interior, Indian Arts and Crafts Board

D. J. Holmes. "Adam and Eve", detail, ivory carving—sperm whale tooth, 4½" x 2½". *Courtesy, Artist*

June Schwarcz. Bowl, electro-plated champlevé and enamel, 6⅛" x 4½". *Courtesy, Artist*

Gary Barlow. "Tribal", stitchery, weaving, beads and feathers. *Collection, Artist*

Detail. *Photos: Graphic Services, Wright State University. Courtesy, Artist*

Arline M. Fisch. "Morrocan Memory", beads, silver and amber, 1971, bead diam., 1½". *Courtesy, Artist*

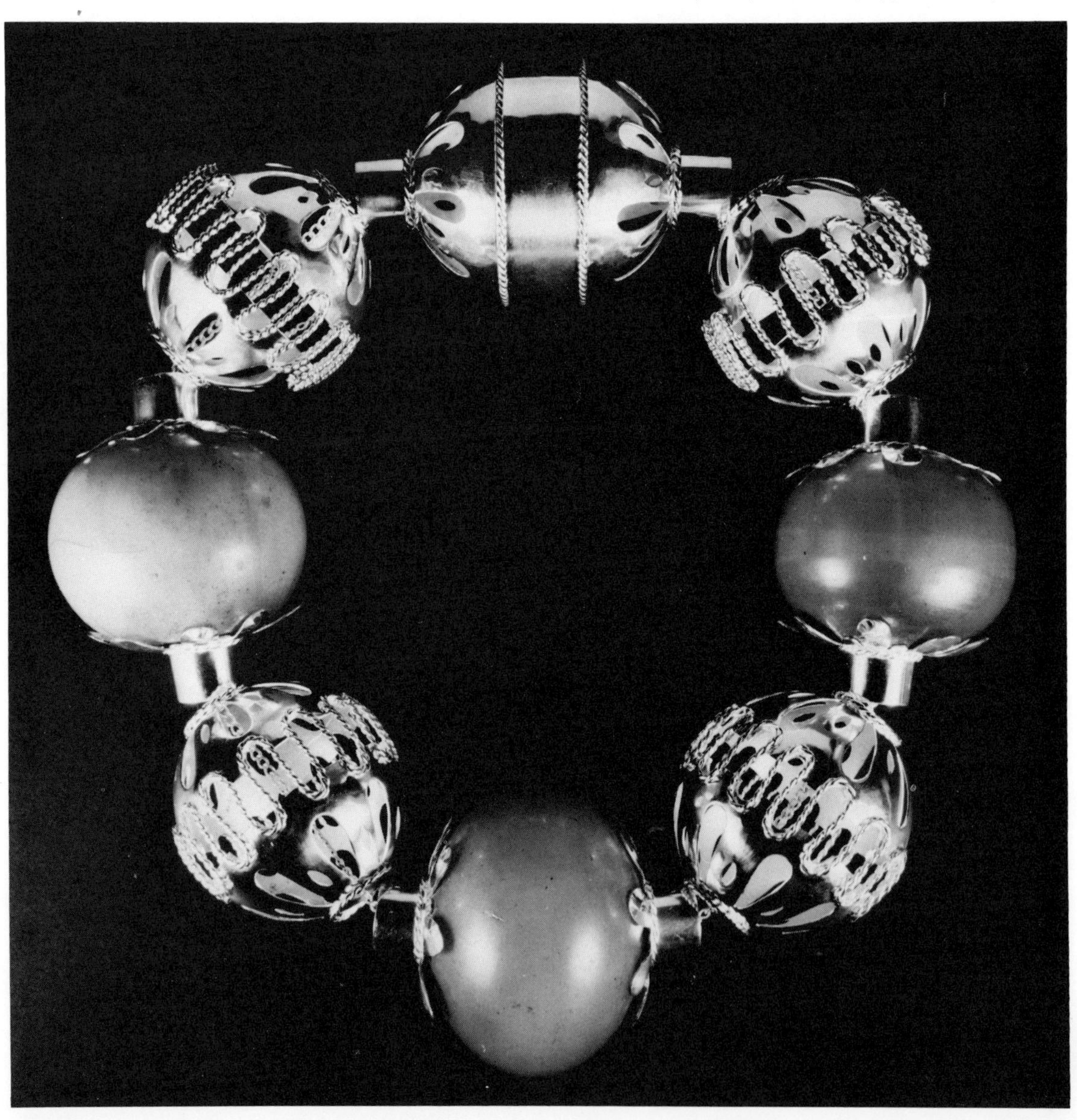

Margaret Sussman. Silver Bowl. *Photo: Erich Vogel. Courtesy, Artist*

D. J. Holmes. "Dante and the Eagle", 4′ x 2′2″ x 6¾″, from an illustration by Gustave Dore, a carved representation done in multiple lamination; basswood, black walnut, Philippine mahogany, teak and frame in sugar pine. *Courtesy, Artist*

June Schwarcz. Bowl, etched, and enameled, 11¾″ x 9¼″. *Collection, Museum of Contemporary Crafts, New York. Courtesy, Artist*

Renie B. Adams, "Gray Still Life with a Constructed Light Source". Stitchery on a crocheted form, cotton, 7″ x 8½″ x 2″. *Courtesy, Artist*

Renie B. Adams. "Basket". Crocheted cotton, ht. 13″, diam. 11″. *Courtesy, Artist*

Suggested Pictorial Reference Books

GENERAL ART

Arnheim, Rudolf. *Art and Visual Perception*, University of California Press, Berkeley, Cal., 1954.

Artz, Frederick. *From the Renaissance to Romanticism*, University of Chicago Press, Chicago, 1962.

Birren, Faber. *Principles of Color*, Reinhold Book Corporation, New York, 1969.

Braun, Julie. *Art, the Image of the West*, Pantheon Books, New York, 1952.

Cheney, Sheldon. *A New World History of Art*, Viking Press, New York, 1956.

Elsen, Albert Edward. *Purposes of Art*, Holt, Rinehart and Winston, New York, 1967.

Gardner, Helen. *Art Through the Ages*, 4th ed., Harcourt, Brace and World, New York, 1962.

Gombrich, Ernst. *The Story of Art*, Phaidon Press, London, 1966.

Halliday, Frank Ernest. *An Illustrated Cultural History of England*, Viking Press, New York, 1967.

Itten, Johannes. *The Art of Color*, Reinhold Book Corporation, New York, 1961.

Janson, H. W. *History of Art*, Harry N. Abrams, New York, 1966.

Lindemann, Gottfried. *History of German Art*, Frederick A. Praeger, New York, 1971.

Malraux, André. *Museum Without Walls*, Doubleday and Company, Garden City, New York, 1967.

Myers, Bernard, *Art and Civilization*, 2nd ed., McGraw-Hill Book Company, New York, 1967.

Payne, Robert. *The World of Art*, Doubleday and Company, Garden City, New York, 1972.

Read, Herbert Edward. *The Meaning of Art*, 3rd ed., Pitman Publishing Corporation, New York, 1951.

Reinach, Salomon. *Apollo: An Illustrated Manual of the History of Art Throughout the Ages*, Charles Scribner's Sons, New York, 1924.

Taylor, Francis Henry. *Fifteen Centuries of Art*, Harper & Bros., New York, 1960.

Upjohn, Everard M., Wingert, Paul S. and Mahler, Jane Gaston. *History of World Art*, 2nd ed., Oxford University Press, New York, 1958.

PRE-HISTORIC ART

Bandi, Hans-Georg. *The Art of the Stone Age*, Crown, New York, 1961.

Brown, Gerard. *Art of the Cave Dwellers*, Murray, London, 1928.

Forman, W. *Pre-Historic Art*, Spring Books, London, 1956.

Kuhn, Herbert. *Rock Pictures in Europe*, Essential Books, New York, 1956.

Torbriigge, Walter. *Pre-Historic European Art*, Harry N. Abrams, New York, 1968.

ANCIENT ART—EGYPT

Aldred, Cyril. *Middle Kingdom Art in Ancient Egypt*, Tiranti, London, 1950.

Carter, Howard. *The Tomb of Tutankhamen*, E. P. Dutton, New York, 1972.

Davies, N. M. *Ancient Egyptian Paintings*, Oxford University Press, Chicago, 1936.

Lange, K. and Hirmer, M. *Egypt: Architecture, Sculpture and Painting in 3000 Years*, Phaidon, New York, 1968.

Mekhitarian, A. *Egyptian Painting*, Skira, Geneva, 1954.

Murray, Margaret Alice. *The Splendor That was Egypt*, Frederick A. Praeger, New York, 1969.

Poulsen, Vagn. *Egyptian Art*, New York Graphic Society, Greenwich, Conn., 1968.

Ranke, H. *Masterpieces of Egyptian Art*, Allen, London, 1951.

Woldering, Irmgard. *The Art of Egypt*, Crown, New York, 1963.

———. *Gods, Men and Pharoahs*, Harry N. Abrams, New York, 1967.

ANCIENT ART—THE NEAR EAST

Frankfort, Henri. *The Art and Architecture of the Ancient Orient*, Penguin Books, Baltimore, Md., 1969.

Lloyd, Seton. *The Art of the Ancient Near East*, Praeger, New York, 1961.

Margueron, Jean-Claude. *Mesopotamia*, World Publishing Company, Cleveland, Ohio, 1965.

Moortjat, Anton. *The Art of Ancient Mesopotamia*, Phaidon, London, 1969.

Smith, Joseph. *Tombs, Temples and Ancient Art*, Oklahoma, 1956.

Vierya, Maurice. *Hittite Art*, Transatlantic, London, 1955.

Wolf, Walther. *The Origins of Western Art: Egypt, Mesopotamia and the Aegean*, Universe Books, New York, 1971.

Woolley, Leonard. *The Development of Sumerina Art*, W. W. Norton, London, 1935.

Zervos, Christian. *L'Art de la Mesopotamie*, Hennessey, Paris, 1935.

BYZANTINE ART AND THE MEDIEVAL ERA

Allen, John. *Celtic Art*, Metheun, London, 1904.

Aubert, Marcel. *Gothic Cathedrals of France and their Treasures*, Kaye, London, 1959.
Beckwith, John. *The Art of Constantinople*, Phaidon, New York, 1961.
———. *Early Medieval Art*, Frederick A. Praeger, New York, 1964.
Bieler, Ludwig. *Ireland: Harbinger of the Middle Ages*, Oxford University Press, New York, 1953.
Bovini, Giuseppe. *Ravenna Mosaics*, Harry N. Abrams, Greenwich, Conn., 1956.
Dalton, Ormonde M. *Byzantine Art and Architecture*, Dover Publications, New York, 1961.
Demus, Otto. *Byzantine Art and the West*, New York University Press, New York, 1970.
Dolling, Regine and Backes, Magnus. *Art of the Dark Ages*, Harry N. Abrams, New York 1971.
Duby, Georges. *The Europe of the Cathedrals*, Skira, Geneva, 1966.
Durant, G. M. *Discovering Medieval Art*, G. Bell, London, 1960.
Edgar, Anthony. *Romanesque Frescoes*, Princeton, Princeton, N.J., 1951.
Evans, Joan. *Art in Medieval France*, Oxford University Press, New York, 1952.
———. *English Art*, 1307–1461, Oxford, 1949.
Focillon, Henri. *The Art of the West in the Middle Ages*, Phaidon, New York, 1963.
Gantner, Joseph and Pobe, Marcel. *The Glory of Romanesque Art*, Vanguard Press, New York, 1956.
Garrison, Edward. *Italian Romanesque Panel Painting*, Olschki, Florence, 1949.
Grabar, Andre. *The Art of the Byzantine Empire*, Crown, New York, 1966.
Hofstatter, Hans Hellmut. *Art of the Late Middle Ages*, Harry N. Abrams, New York, 1968.
Kendrick, Thomas. *Late Saxon and Viking Art*, Barnes and Noble, New York, 1949.
Lowrie, Walter. *Art in the Early Church*, Peter Smith, New York, 1947.
Morey, Charles Rufus. *Early Christian Art*, Princeton University Press, Princeton, N.J., 1953.
———. *Medieval Art*, W. W. Norton, New York, 1942.
Rice, David Talbot. *Byzantine Art*, Penguin Books, Harmondsworth, 1968.
Saunders, Elfrida. *History of English Art in the Middle Ages*, Clarendon, Oxford, 1932.
Swarzinski, Hanns. *Monuments of Romanesque Art*, University of Chicago Press, Chicago, 1967.
Verone, Paolo. *The Art of Europe: The Dark Ages from Theodoric to Charlemagne*, Crown, New York, 1968.
Zarnecki, George. *Romanesque Art*, Universe Books, New York, 1971.

ANCIENT ART—THE AEGEAN, ETRURIA, GREECE AND ROME

Bassert, Theodore. *The Art of Ancient Crete*, Zwemmer, London, 1937.
Becatti, Giovanni. *Tht Art of Ancient Greece and Rome*, Harry N. Abrams, New York, 1967.
Bloch, Raymond. *Etruscan Art*, New York Graphic Society, Greenwich, Conn., 1966.
Buschor, Ernst. *Greek Vase Painting*, Argonaut, London, 1921.
Evans, Arthur. *The Palace of Minos*, Biblo, London, 1935.
Giglioli, Giulio. *L'Arte Etrusca*, Treves, Milan, 1935.
Hafner, Germain. *The Art of Rome, Etruria and Magna Graecia*, Harry N. Abrams, New York, 1971.

Kjellberg, Ernst. *Greek and Roman Art*, Apollo, New York, 1968.

Lukas, Jan. *Pompeii and Herculaneum*, Spring Books, London, 1966.

Marinatos, Spyridon. *Crete and Mycenae*, Harry N. Abrams, New York, 1967.

Matz, Friedrich. *The Art of Crete and Early Greece*, Crown, New York, 1962.

Pfuhl, Ernst. *Masterpieces of Greek Drawing and Painting*, Argonaut, New York, 1955.

Reverdin, Olivier. *Crete and Its Treasures*, Viking Press, New York, 1961.

Richardson, Emeline Hill. *The Etruscans: Their Art and Civilization*, University of Chicago Press, Chicago, 1964.

Richter, Gisela M. A. *Perspective in Greek and Roman Art*, Phaidon, New York, 1970.

Riis, Paul. *An Introduction to Etruscan Art*, Munksgaard, Copenhagen, 1953.

Strong, Eugene. *Art in Ancient Rome*, Charles Scribner's Sons, New York, 1928.

Swindler, May. *Ancient Painting*, Yale University Press, New Haven, Conn., 1929.

THE RENAISSANCE, BAROQUE AND ROCOCO

Adhemar, Jean. *French Drawing of the Sixteenth Century*, Vanguard Press, New York, 1955.

Bazin, Germaine. *Baroque and Rococo*, Frederick A. Praeger, New York, 1964.

Benesch, Otto. *The Art of the Renaissance in Northern Europe*, Archon Books, Hamden, Conn., 1964.

Berensen, Bernard. *The Italian Painters of the Renaissance*, Phaidon, New York, 1952.

Chastel, Andre. *The Flowering of the Italian Renaissance*, Odyssey Press, New York, 1965.

Editors of Horizon Magazine. *The Horizon Book of the Renaissance*, American Heritage Publishing Corp., New York, 1961.

Hartt, Frederick. *History of the Italian Renaissance*, Harry N. Abrams, New York, 1969.

Hay, Denys, Ed., *The Age of the Renaissance*, McGraw-Hill Book Corp., New York, 1967.

Haskell, Francis. *Patrons and Painters*, Alfred A. Knopf, New York, 1963.

Hempel, Eberhardt. *Baroque Art and Architecture in Central Europe*, Penguin Books, Baltimore, Md., 1965.

Mather, Frank. *Western European Painting of the Renaissance*, Cooper Square, New York, 1948.

Milne, James Lees. *Baroque in Italy*, Batsford, London, 1960.

Pignatti, Terisio. *The Age of Rococo*, P. Hamlyn, London, 1969.

Sewter, A. C. *Baroque and Rococo*, Harcourt, Brace, Jovanovich, New York, 1972.

Vasari, Giorgio. *The Lives of the Artists*, Abridged and Edited by Betty Burroughs, Simon & Schuster, New York, 1946.

MODERN ART

Barr, Alfred H., Jr. *Masters of Modern Art*, Arno Press, New York, 1961.

———. *Picasso, Fifty Years of his Art*, Arno Press, New York, 1966.

Bowness, Allan. *Impressionism and Post Impressionism*, Harcourt, Brace & World, New York, 1965.

Cooper, Douglas. *The Cubist Epoch*, Phaidon, New York, 1971.
Dorival, Bernard. *Twentieth Century Painters*, Universe Books, New York, 1958.
Haftman, Werner. *Painting in the Twentieth Century*, Frederick A. Praeger, New York, 1965.
Huyghe, René, Ed. *Encyclopedia of Modern Art from 1800 to the Present Day*, Putnam, New York, 1965.
Lynton, Norbert. *The Modern World*, McGraw-Hill Book Co., New York, 1965.
Museum of Modern Art. *Cubism and Abstract Art*, Museum of Modern Art, New York, 1936.
Raynal, Maurice. *Modern Painting*, Skira, Geneva, 1960.
Read, Herbert Edward. *Art Now*, Pitman Publishing Corp., New York, 1968.
———. *The Philosophy of Modern Art*, Horizon Press, New York, 1953.
Rewald, John. *Post-Impressionism from Van Gogh to Gauguin*, Museum of Modern Art, New York, 1956.
Selz, Jean. *Modern Sculpture*, Braziller, New York, 1963.
Soby, James Thrall. *Contemporary Painters*, Museum of Modern Art, New York, 1948.

ISLAMIC ART

Akurgal, Ekrem. *Treasures of Turkey*, Skira, Geneva, 1966.
Coomaraswamy, Ananda Kentish. *The Arts and Crafts of India and Ceylon*, Farrar, New York, 1964.
———. *History of Indian and Indonesian Art*, Peter Smith, New York, 1927.
Ghirshman, Roman. *The Arts of Ancient Iran*, Golden Press, New York, 1964.
———. *Persian Art*, Golden Press, New York, 1962.
Goetz, Hermann. *The Art of India*, Dover Publications, New York, 1965.
———. *Five Thousand Years of Indian Art*, Crown Publishing Co., New York, 1964.
Grube, Ernst J. *The World of Islam*, McGraw-Hill Book Corp., New York, 1967.
Kiihnel, Ernst. *Islamic Art and Architecture*, Cornell University Press, Ithaca, N.Y., 1966.
———. *The Minor Arts of Islam*, Cornell University Press, Ithaca, N.Y., 1971.
Parrot, André. *The Arts of Assyria*, Golden Press, New York, 1961.
Pope, Arthur Upham. *Masterpieces of Persian Art*, The Dryden Press, New York, 1945.
Stewart, Desmond Stirling, and others. *Early Islam*, Time-Life Books, New York, 1967.

FAR EASTERN ART

Akiyama, Terukazu. *The Arts of China*, Kodansha, Palo Alto, Cal., 1968.
———. *Japanese Painting*, Skira, Lausanne, 1972.
Ashton, Leigh. *Chinese Art*, Faber & Faber, Beechhurst, 1953.
Chang, Yee. *Chinese Calligraphy*, Cambridge, Mass., 1954.
Dye, Daniel S. *A Grammar of Chinese Lattice*, Harvard University Press, Cambridge, Mass., 1949.
Feddersen, Martin. *Japanese Decorative Art*, Yoseloff, New York, 1962.
Fenollosa, Ernest. *Epochs of Chinese and Japanese Art*, Peter Smith, New York, 1963.
Hobson, Robert L. *Chinese Art*, Somerset, London, 1952.

Jenys, R. Soame and Jourdain, Margaret, *Chinese Export Art*, Charles Scribner's Sons, New York, 1950.

Jenyns, R. Soame and Watson, William. *Chinese Art: The Minor Arts*, Universe Books, New York, 1965.

Kim, Chewon. *Treasures of Korean Art*, Harry N. Abrams, New York, 1966.

Lane, Richard. *Masters of the Japanese Print: Their World and Their Work*, Doubleday & Company, Garden City, New York, 1962.

Lee, Sherman E. *A History of Far Eastern Art*, Harry N. Abrams, New York, 1964.

Medley, Margaret. *A Handbook of Chinese Art for Collectors and Students*, Horizon Press, New York, 1965.

Munsterberg, Hugo. *Art of the Far East*, Harry N. Abrams, New York, 1968.

———. *Zen and Oriental Art*, Charles R. Tuttle, Rutland, Vt., 1965.

Strange, Edward. *Chinese Lacquer*, Benn, London, 1926.

Swann, Peter Charles. *Art of China, Korea and Japan*, Frederick A. Praeger, New York, 1963.

Yashiro, Yukio. *Two Thousand Years of Japanese Art*, Edited by Peter C. Swann, Harry N. Abrams, New York, 1958.

FOLK ARTS

Adam, Leonhard. *Primitive Art*, Barnes & Noble, Middlesex, 1949.

Appleton, Leroy. *Indian Art of the Americas*, Charles Scribner's Sons, New York, 1950.

Beier, Ulli. *Contemporary Art in Africa*, Northwest University Press, New York, 1968.

Bliss, Robert. *Pre-Colombian Art*, Phaidon, New York, 1957.

Boas, Franz. *Primitive Art*, Dover Publications, New York, 1955.

Bossert, Helmuth T. *Folk Art of Asia, Africa and the Americas*, Frederick A. Praeger, New York, 1964.

———. *Folk Art of Primitive Peoples: Six Hundred Decorative Motifs in Color*, Frederick A. Praeger, New York, 1956.

Buhler, Alfred. *The Art of the South Seas Islands*, Crown, New York, 1962.

Castedo, Leopoldo. *A History of Latin American Art and Architecture*, Frederick A. Praeger, New York, 1969.

Christensen, Erwin O. *The Index of American Design*, Macmillan, New York, 1950.

Fraser, Douglas. *Primitive Art*, Doubleday & Company, Garden City, N.Y., 1962.

Gardi, René. *African Crafts and Craftsmen*, Van Nostrand Reinhold, New York, 1970.

Griaule, Marcel. *Folk Arts of Black Africa*, Tudor Publishing Co., New York, 1950.

Keleman, Pal. *Art of the Americas*, Thomas Y. Crowell, New York, 1969.

Lloyd, Joan Barklay. *African Animals in Renaissance Literature*, Clarendon Press, Oxford, 1971.

Lowie, Robert. *Indians of the Plains*, Museum of Natural History, New York, 1954.

Maury, Curt. *Folk Origins of Indian Art*, Columbia University Press, New York, 1969.

Monti, Franco. *African Masks*, P. Hamlyn, London, 1969.

Newton, Douglas. *Art Styles of the Papuan Gulf*, Museum of Primitive Art, New York, 1961.

———. *New Guinea Art in the Collection of the Museum of Primitive Art*, Museum of Primitive Art, New York, 1967.

Philips, W. J. *Maori Carving Illustrated*, A. H. and A. W. Reed, Wellington, New Zealand, 1955.

Schmalenbach, Werner *African Art*, The Macmillan Co., New York, 1954.

Segy, Ladislas. *African Art Studies*, Wittenborn, New York, 1956.

———. *African Sculpture Speaks*, Hill & Wang, New York, 1969.

Smith, Bradley. *Mexico, A History in Art*, Harper & Row, New York, 1968.

Smith, Bernard. *European Vision and the South Pacific*, Clarendon Press, Oxford, 1960.

Sourek, Karel. *Folk Art in Pictures*, Spring Books, London, 1960.

Spinden, Herbert J. *Maya Art and Civilization*, Falcon's Wing Press, New York, 1957.

Trowell, Margaret. *African and Oceanic Art*, Harry N. Abrams, New York, 1968.

———. *African Design*, Frederick A. Praeger, 3rd ed., New York, 1970.

Ubbelohde-Doering, Heinrich. *Art of Ancient Peru*, Frederick A. Praeger, New York, 1952.

Wassing, René S. *African Art*, Harry N. Abrams, New York, 1968.

Wingert, Paul S. and Linton, Ralph. *Arts of the South Seas*, Museum of Modern Art, New York, 1946.

Wingert, Paul S. *Primitive Art, Its Traditions and Styles*, Oxford University Press, New York, 1962.

DECORATIVE ARTS AND CRAFTS

Anthony, Edgar Waterman. *A History of Mosaics*, Hacker Art Books, New York, 1968.

Amaya, Mario. *Art Nouveau*, E. P. Dutton, New York, 1966.

Audsley, W. & G. *Designs and Patterns from Historic Ornament*, Dover Publications, New York, 1968.

Ball, Katherine. *Decorative Motives of Oriental Art*, Hacker Art Books, New York, 1927.

Barnard, Julian. *Victorian Ceramic Tiles*, New York Graphic Society, Greenwich, Conn., 1972.

Bing, Samuel. *Artistic America, Tiffany Glass and Art Nouveau*, Massachusetts Institute of Technology Press, Cambridge, Mass., 1970.

Boger, Louise. *Dictionary of Antiques and the Decorative Arts*, Charles Scribner's Sons, New York, 1957.

Bossert, Theodor. *Ornament in Applied Art*, Weyhe, New York, 1924.

Brazer, Esther. *Early American Decoration*, Pond-Ekberg, Springfield, Mass., 1947.

Day, Lewis F., *Pattern Design*, Charles Scribner's Sons, New York, 1933.

Dickason, David H. *The Daring Young Men: Story of the American Pre-Raphaelites*, Bloomington, Ind., 1953.

Dilley, Arthur. *Oriental Rugs and Carpets*, Lippincott, New York, 1931.

Dresser, Christopher. *Principles of Decorative Design*, 3rd ed., Charles Scribner's Sons, New York, 1959.

Eberlein, Harold D. and Ramsdell, Roger W. *The Practical Book of Chinaware*, Lippincott, New York, 1948.

Editors of American Fabrics Magazine, *American Fabrics Encyclopedia of Textiles*, Prentice-Hall, Englewood Cliffs, N.J., 1972.

Entwistle, E. A. *The Book of Wallpaper*, Textile Books, London, 1954.

Evans, John. *A Study of Ornament in Western Europe from* 1180–1900, Clarendon, Oxford, 1931.

Faraday, Cornelia. *European and American Carpets and Rugs*, Dean-Hicks, Grand Rapids, Mich., 1929.

Fischer, Peter. *Mosaic, History and Technique*, McGraw-Hill Book Co., New York, 1971.

Gaunt, William. *The Pre-Raphaelite Dream*, Schocken Books, New York, 1966.

Gillon, Edmund V., Jr. *An Anthology of Design and Illustration from the Studio*, Dover Publications, New York, 1969.

———. *Early New England Gravestone Rubbings*, Dover Publications, New York, 1966.

Glazier, Richard. *A Manual of Historic Ornament*, Tower, New York, 1948.

Grover, Ray & Lee. *Art Glass Nouveau*, Charles R. Tuttle, Rutland, Vermont, 1967.

Hanley, Hope. *Needlepoint in America*, Charles Scribner's Sons, New York, 1969.

Hatton, Richard G. *Handbook of Plant and Floral Ornament from Early Herbals*, Dover Publications, New York, 1960.

Henderson, Philip. *William Morris, His Life, Work and Friends*, McGraw-Hill Book Co., New York, 1967.

Hilton, Timothy. *The Pre-Raphaelites*, Harry N. Abrams, New York, 1970.

Honey, William. *European Ceramic Art from the Middle Ages to* 1815, Faber & Faber, London, 1952.

Hornung, Clarence P. *Hornung's Handbook of Designs and Devices*, 2nd ed., Dover Pub., New York, 1946.

———. *Treasury of American Design*, Harry N. Abrams, New York, 1972.

Jacques, Renata and Flemming, Ernst. *Encyclopedia of Textiles*, Frederick A. Praeger, New York, 1958.

Jessen, Ellen, *Ancient Peruvian Textile: Design in Modern Stitchery*, Van Nostrand Reinhold, New York, 1972.

Jones, Owen. *A Grammar of Ornament* (1856), repub., Van Nostrand Reinhold, New York, 1973.

Kendrick, A. *Handwoven Carpets, Oriental and European*, Dover Publication, London, 1922.

Lane, Maggie. *More Needlepoint by Design*, Charles Scribner's Sons, New York, 1972.

Lichten, Frances M. *Decorative Art of Victoria's Era, Charles Scribner's Sons*, New York, 1950.

Madsen, Stephan T. *Sources of Art Nouveau*, Wittenborn, New York, 1956.

McClelland, Nancy V. *Historic Wallpapers*, Lippincott, Philadelphia, 1924.

McClinton, Katherine Morrison. *Art Deco: A Guide for Collectors*, Clarkson Potter, New York, 1972.

Menten, Theodore, ed. *Art Nouveau and Early Art Deco Type and Design, from the Roman Scherer Catalogue*, Dover Publications, New York, 1972.

Meyer, Franz. *A Handbook of Ornament*, Dover Publications, Chicago, 1945.

Minneapolis Institute of Arts. *The World of Art Deco*, E. P. Dutton, New York, 1971.

Mirow, Gregory. *A Treasury of Design for Artists and Craftsmen*, Dover Publications, New York, 1969.

Pevsner, Nikolaus. *Pioneers of Modern Design from William Morris to Walter Gropius*, Museum of Modern Art, dist. Simon & Schuster, New York, 1949.

Powers, Harry. *The Art of Mosaic*, The University Prints, Newton, Mass., 1938.

Rheims, Maurice. *The Flowering of Art Nouveau*, Harry N. Abrams, New York, 1966.

Sabine, Ellen S. *Early American Decorative Patterns and How to Paint Them*, Van Nostrand, Princeton, N.J., 1962.

Safford, Carleton L. and Bishop, Robert. *America's Quilts and Coverlets*, E. P. Dutton, New York, 1972.

Schiffer, Margaret B. *Historical Needlework of Pennsylvania*, Charles Scribner's Sons, New York, 1968.

Schmutzler, Maurice. *Art Nouveau*, Harry N. Abrams, New York, 1962.

Short, Eiran. *Embroidery and Fabric College*, Charles Scribner's & Sons, New York, 1973.

Somer, Robert. *The Lost Art, A Survey of One Thousand Years of Stained Glass*, Wittenborn, New York, 1954.

Steegman, John. *Victorian Taste*, Massachusetts Institute of Technology Press, Cambridge, Mass., 1971.

Thompson, Paul R. *The Work of William Morris*, Viking Press, New York, 1967.

Wakefield, Hugh. *Victorian Pottery*, Nelson, New York, 1962.

Waring, Janet. *Early American Stencil Decorations*, Century House, Watkins Glen, N.Y., 1937.

Watkinson, Ray. *Pre-Raphaelite Art and Design*, New York Graphic Society, Greenwich, Conn., 1970.

———. *William Morris as Designer*, Van Nostrand Reinhold, New York, 1967.

Westlake, Nat. *A History of Design in Stained Glass*, Parker, London, 1894.

Weibel, Adéle Coulin. *Two Thousand Years of Textiles*, Hacker Art Books, New York, 1952.

Wiczyk, Arlene, ed. *A Treasury of Needlework Projects from Godey's Lady's Book*, Arco, New York, 1972.

Wilson, Erica. *Erica Wilson's Embroidery Book*, Charles Scribner's Sons, New York, 1973.

Winchester, Alice and the staff of Antiques Magazine. *The Antiques Treasury of Furniture and Other Decorative Arts*, E. P. Dutton, Colonial Williamsburg, 1962.

Yates, Raymond. *Early American Crafts and Hobbies*, W. Funk, New York, 1954.

Index